"Newgotiation"
For Public Administration Professionals

D1452966

"NEWGOTIATION"
FOR PUBLIC ADMINISTRATION PROFESSIONALS
Collaboration Framing Negotiation©

YANN DUZERT, PH.D.
FRANK V. ZERUNYAN, J.D.

Yann Duzert, Ph.D. Professor, Rennes School of Business, France; Visiting Professor University of Southern California; CEO of Newgotiation, Inc. consultant and coach

Frank Vram Zerunyan, J.D. LL.D. (hc) Professor of the Practice of Governance and Director of Executive Education, University of Southern California Sol Price School of Public Policy; Three term Mayor and Council Member, City of Rolling Hills Estates, California.

"NEWGOTIATION" FOR PUBLIC ADMINISTRATION PROFESSIONALS
Collaboration Framing Negotiation©

Yann Duzert, Ph.D.
Frank V. Zerunyan, J.D.

Published by:

Vandeplas Publishing, LLC – July 2019

801 International Parkway, 5th Floor
Lake Mary, FL. 32746
USA

www.vandeplaspublishing.com

ISBN 978-1-60042-500-4

CONTENTS

We spend 80% of our life negotiating for something. According to The Carnegie Institute of Technology, 85% of our financial success is attributable to our personality and skills in "human engineering." These skills, among others, include communication, self-confidence, initiative, empathy, negotiation and leadership. By contrast, only 15% of our financial success is due to technical skills, even though we spend many years of education to acquire them. While we do not underrate the importance of education, Nobel Prize winning Israeli-American psychologist Daniel Kahneman found that people prefer to conduct business with a person they like and respect rather than a person they dislike or do not trust, even if that person is offering a better product at a lower price.

In a study conducted by Hay/McBer Research and Innovation Group, emotional intelligence, which is rich in human skills, outpaced technical intelligence. At L'Oréal, sales agents selected on the basis of their strong emotional intelligence significantly outsold sales persons selected under old selection processes. In a national insurance company, insurance sales agents with strong emotional competencies outsold their weaker counterparts at more than 2 to 1. In a large beverage firm, 50% of new hires left within two years, primarily because of poor performance. When the firm began hiring based on a new criterion using emotional intelligence, only 6% left in two years.

According to Forbes, Fortune 500 companies have a low rate of success in implementing projects. Out of 100 projects only 30 are implemented. Seventy fail for lack of human skills, such as leadership and poor negotiation skills between internal departments. According to Harvard's Negotiation Program, 95% of American executives have never received formal education of negotiation or conflict resolution.

Newgotiation for Public Administration Professionals conveys practical tools for Public Administration Professionals, executives, managers and professionals from the public sector to improve performance and relationships in this highly competitive multi sectoral and global marketplace. Our methodological approach to negotiation emphasizes the physiological conditions in the interaction between different types of actors with varied levels of power.

Newgotiation for Public Administration Professionals explores pedagogical instruments for Public Administration Professionals to focus on collaboration, relationships and trust. Throughout our "Newgotiation" process, there are moments of reflection alternating with moments of action, allowing each participant to craft a path to a meaningful win/win. Our methodology is all about identifying potential problems, crafting solutions and structuring value creation and value distribution based on organizational priorities, values and ethics. In order to improve the training pedagogy among Public Administration Professionals, we created our 4-10-10 Technique of Newgotiation as a unifying dialect, which helps public and private organizations to speak the same language to cut a better deal. Armed with the same lexicon of ingredients everyone can achieve better negotiation skills building reputation and trust. Newgotiation is a process that can be taught. With our contributions in this book, as well as our training modules across the globe, we hope to create better environments for intersectoral collaborations and negotiations.

INTRODUCTION AND ACKNOWLEDGMENTS

This short, readable book offers an insight to negotiating for Public Administration Professionals by developing both academic and practical topics that directly impact the daily life, behavior, comportment, habits and skills of successful public servants in the art and science of negotiation. Academic books, articles and some practice manuals have been written on the single thematic subject of "Negotiation." However, none that we could find address Public Administration Professionals in the context of public administration, especially highlighting "governance" as opposed to "government." The former term implies that the development and implementation of public policy and administration is increasingly shared among a plurality of actors. We use this topic of governance, and more importantly "collaborative governance" to frame our subject matter, which we call "Newgotiation." Governance requires a different mindset with collaborative effort to search for the common good. Successful governance is all about the quest for the win/win, which mirrors our new process for negotiations that we explore in this book. We call this new process "Newgotiation."

We are professors of the practice of governance and negotiation. We care about the exploration and application of the best possible scholarship and best available practices in public administration and management. Civic innovations created in the ivory towers of our research universities must have reason and function in our town squares around the world. We believe public service is a noble calling and for the clear majority of public servants a distinguished effort to serve one's own community, city, district, county, state or country. Earning the public's trust is a special feeling for all who serve in public office especially in elected office. Unfortunately, in recent years we have witnessed the degradation of that trust with the most egregious displays of conduct unbecoming a public leader.

This book comes at a time when citizens locally, nationally and globally are demanding better governance, greater sectoral participation in public affairs and enhanced integrity and accountability of their leaders in all forms of negotiations. We write this book with the intention of orienting Public Administration

Professionals 1) to focus on good and ethical governance practices, 2) to adapt the new paradigm of collaboration and consensus building 3) to recognize worst and best negotiators and their tactics 4) to review challenges and opportunities to achieve "integration" of interests or the "win/win" 5) to create value for the people they represent 6) to distribute value to sustain a long term and viable relationship with negotiating partners, and 7) to facilitate collaboration through leadership.

The orientation we describe is a new perspective providing framework clearly based in normative theory but at the same time is suggestive of areas for empirical analysis plainly written for Public Administration Professionals around the world. We are not naïve enough to think that we provide in this book a magic or "silver bullet" to deal with all negotiations. We simply attempt to help the public leader find the collaborative frame and achieve the often desired but hardly obtained win/win result. Our hope is to guide the public leader to better governance and public service.

This book is the culmination of our work over 18 years at the Fundação Getúlio Vargas (FGV), Rio de Janeiro, in collaboration with our colleagues at the University of Southern California Sol Price School of Public Policy (USC). Together we built a modern method of negotiation adapted to Public Administration Professionals, which we named "Newgotiation for Public Administration Professionals." A new style, a new mentality, a new relationship to leadership in the context of public administration.

The underlying method has been published in numerous academic seminars and is already discussed in 16 books published by 3 Nobel laureates, our colleagues from FGV, USC, Harvard University, Massachusetts Institute of Technology (MIT), Stanford University, University Institute of Lisbon (ISCTE), Escola Superior de Guerra, Escola Superior de Magistratura, École Supérieure des Sciences Économiques et Commerciales (ESSEC), École Supérieure de Commerce de Paris (ESCP), Universidade Federal do Rio de Janeiro (UFRJ) and Universidade do Estado do Rio de Janeiro (UERJ). This method is based on the Complex Negotiation Matrix called the 4-10-10 Technique, which is taught to more than one million people worldwide, including Brazil, China, France, Italy, Mexico, and the United States of America.

Research shows that we spend more than 80% of our lives negotiating, with our family, our neighbors, our colleagues, our customers, suppliers, shareholders and our governments. The word "Negotiation" in Latin—"Nega Otium"—means denying leisure, free time or pleasure. This definition implies that we devote the greater part of our lives to an occupation, a business or activity, which is ineffectual. Often, we describe negotiation as an arm-wrestling contest, a fight or a war. The corporate world as well as the general public continues to buy Sun Tsu's book "The Art of War." In that book, negotiation is described as a tactic of war, a strategy of chess, a frame where one wins and the other loses. Thus, the traditional pedagogy of negotiation focuses on belligerent strategies, manipulations and games of persuasion. Traditional negotiation is defined as a game of power, influence and political tactics. Alas, in the modern world, this old school representation of negotiation is what Kodak is to the iPhone—an old obsolete impotent rival.

Modern 21st century public organizations can no longer decide rationally on the basis of authority and power much less relying on obsolete tools. A local, state or federal government has an 80% chance of being subjected to a major crisis by failing to agree. This fragility requires a different frame than competition, fight or war. Public organizations can no longer afford decisions based on the rationality of the majority. The games of power, the rules of the majority are not always sufficient to execute decisions. A minority often can block a decision. A minority can impose rules, norms and positions of power. The strength of social networks places the individual at the heart of negotiation. David vs. Goliath in the new digital era reveals the importance of transparency, integrity, reputation and trust. These are skills and characteristics shared in governance, negotiation and leadership.

An opaque structure frozen in time, where the various departments of the organization operate in a silo no longer functional. Public Administration Professionals today value a new style of negotiation based on moral elegance, collaborative governance and sustainable development. Public Administration Professionals seek to change their culture to emulate the success of Silicon Valley, by de- bureaucratizing, decompartmentalizing through collaboration and innovation. A study found that organizations that have graceful habits, cordial service and long-term thinking, enjoy the greatest margins and sustainable futures. Operational management is strategic. However, it is not worth much if it is not harmonized with a marketing relationship. President Clinton mentioned at a conference in which we participated that most of the conflicts he had to solve began and ended with the management of identity. The paradigm of negotiation that we address in this book takes into account this triangle of interests, identity and communication. The negotiating theories, namely the interest-based literature established mainly by scholars and practitioners at Harvard, have taken into account some elements of negotiation harmonized to interests. This method, which is now 30 years old, remains effective but incomplete.

We note that this book is rooted in literature, theory, analysis and practice, some of which are reflected by our original work in governance, good decision making and Newgotiation. We see this book as providing theoretical and practical negotiation insight to Public Administration Professionals focusing on the role and responsibility of public leaders both elected and appointed. While our primary direction is for local government leaders, we clearly see applications for any public leader or official in any public office.

We want to acknowledge that we chose not to make this book scholarly in the sense of documenting sources used in great bibliographic detail. We do provide information on relevant authors, book titles and journal articles that make it possible for our readers to readily search for these sources when more detail or information is desired. In fact, we hope that our readers will be stimulated enough to seek more information about the sources we discuss in this book as well as our subject matter.

Finally, we made every effort to compress our discussion to make this book short, to the point and rich in real life examples. Our purpose is to use this book as well as our other training materials to build capacity among our students and Public Administration Professionals. In this regard, we wish to acknowledge our friends and colleagues in academia as well as in public office for their assistance and encouragement to write this book.

We are, also, indebted and grateful for the invaluable contribution of our good friend and colleague Professor Ali Abbas, an accomplished scholar and practitioner of decision analysis, risk analysis and data-based decision making. His discipline in industrial systems engineering and public policy, give him a unique perspective in information theory and practice. His short chapter focuses on the basic elements of decision, along with "reflections on the effects of organizational complexity and incentive structures on the decision-making environment." We find his contribution to this book vital in light of the fact that Newgotiation is all about the right or "helpful frame," as he calls it, in the decision-making process.

Finally, we wish to acknowledge our students who help us research and provide us with an amazing laboratory to test and be tested on our subject matters. As professors in preeminent research universities, we know that the quality of our students directly correlates to our ability to research and educate. Therefore, we thank them for their contributions.

CHAPTER 1:
Context of Collaboration in Governance

We suggest that the field of public administration is experiencing a paradigm shift in the "steering of society" from "government" to "governance." The latter term implies that the development and implementation of public policy are increasingly distributed or shared among a plurality of actors and sectors. Today, public, private, not-for-profit or non-governmental organizations (NGO), and citizens (sometimes called the fourth sector) are much more connected and predisposed to collaborate than ever before. These sectors, organizations or persons—each with their own special interests, motivations, resources and capabilities—are providing unprecedented opportunities to restructure governments to better govern.

Collaborative arrangements today, especially between the sectors, provide for novel approaches to organizing public administration. Perhaps for more than a century, the public, private and not-for-profit sectors developed intra-sectorally but exploited and consumed intersectorally. The hierarchical "silos" they each created generally ignored the other, creating long lasting tensions and breaches of trust. While all three sectors often serve the same constituency (the public), their motivations and intentions are quite different and inconsistent in framework.

The public sector remains the steward and guardian of the rule of law, social justice, the public interest and the provision of "public goods." The private sector on the other hand primarily focuses on profits, private interest and "private goods." These interests and goods compete and at times to the detriment of the other. Ironically, neither can exist without the other. Wall Street is unimaginable without rules and regulations. We have decades of history and examples to illustrate this point. The irresponsible at worst and less thoughtful at best lack of laws and deregulations of savings and loans, the energy sector during the Enron era and the recent mortgage back securities crisis brought the private and public market places to their knees. While regulations and deregulations are matters of debate in the political context, their effects in public administration are clear. Without a well-balanced and fair rule of law, these sectors are incapable of functioning much less collaborating. The following pages discuss collaboration as a topic to orient our Public Administration Professionals in the context of public administration and negotiations that lead to sustainable results.

Our former colleague Warren Bennis clearly articulated, "In a global society, in which timely information is the most important commodity, collaboration is not simply desirable—it is inevitable." Historically, collaborations brought us amazing innovations and projects. In the private sector, collaborations of innovators and skill sets created Apple, Disney, Hewlett Packard and even the movie Star Wars. In the public sector, collaborations facilitated the Lakewood Plan of 1954 in California, allowing municipalities to contract with other governments and sectors for the delivery of special municipal services. These collaborations deliver statutorily defined special municipal services in finance, economy, accounting, engineering, administration and law, creating an efficient system for public administration. For example, in the city of Rolling Hills Estates, California, a city with little over 8,000 residents, waste is collected by Waste Management, a private company. City traffic engineering and legal services are also delivered by the private sector. The Los Angeles County Sheriff Department and Fire Department are the first responders of the city of Rolling Hills Estates, as well as the county of Los Angeles. The city directly employs only 19 people, who primarily manage all these contracts with other governments and the private sector to deliver all needed municipal services in Rolling Hills Estates.

In the not-for-profit or NGO sector, the product RED conceived by U2's Bono and Robert Shriver focuses on the eradication of AIDS from Africa by connecting governments, international organizations and private companies to the mission. Apple, The Gap, Starbucks and others produce "RED" products to donate portions of the proceeds to the mission. Also, a global collaboration sparked by former Ambassador Morgenthau in 1919 created the Red Cross by the Near East Relief Foundation to help the orphans of the first genocide of the 20th Century. The Near East Relief Foundation raised more than 117 million dollars in 1919 for the "starving Armenians."

Today, collaborations require new skills and knowledge. According to the Harvard Business Review (HBR), these new skills require, "far deeper appreciation of societal needs, a greater understanding of the true bases of company productivity, and the ability to collaborate across profit/nonprofit boundaries. And government must learn how to regulate in ways that enable shared value rather than work against it." HBR goes on to explain, "The solution lies in the principle of shared value, which involves creating economic value in a way that also creates value for society by addressing its needs and challenges. Businesses must reconnect company success with social progress. Shared value is not social responsibility, philanthropy, or even sustainability, but a new way to achieve economic success." Aligning this shared value through good decisions and motivations provides our frame for collaborative governance as well as what we call Newgotiation.

The competitive frame (fight or war) of the last century bringing about the breaches of trust are in a state of flux. Tensions built to create winners and losers (also known as "hard power") are being reconsidered and replaced with "smart power." (Note: We discuss "smart power" in later chapters.) The 21st century necessities and the global media-dominated context help ease these tensions and provide a better understanding of each sector vis-à-vis the other, in turn facilitating collaborations not necessarily to feel good but to improve productivity. Demographic changes and preferences of millennials, the largest buying cohort in 2017, refocus our attention to a smaller footprint through a shared economy and convenience through the internet of things.

Over a billion people have smart phones to share things and collaborate. As the financial security of cities weakens and complexity of public administration problems heightens, the need to collaborate with partners that can bring fresh perspective and resources to public administration is magnified. Heightened interest among the tech savvy millennials improve engagement and leverage change. Public agencies are beginning to see the benefit of positioning themselves to align with mission driven high tech non-profits, innovative for-profit organizations and engaged citizens at large to create the tools that enable better governance.

Increasing number of creative innovations provide valuable solutions to the public sector through the creation of simple mobile applications. Code for America (CfA), is a non-profit committed to bringing high-tech programmers together with local governments to solve real world problems. Companies such as Google, ESRI and O'Reilly Media have come together to not only sponsor these innovations but also provide some of the needed human capital to do this good work.

The City of New Orleans partnered with CfA in 2012 to help resolve the slow identification of blighted properties. After hurricane Katrina, the City of New Orleans assisted developers to identify 35,000 abandoned properties. CfA launched BlightStatus, an application that scoured through layers of digital data and offered real time information on blighted properties. This project has since been celebrated as an example of how innovation created and implemented by non-government actors can result in better governance.

Products like Ways, a collaboration among ordinary citizens, is facilitating transportation policy. Nest, HomeKit and Amazon's Alexa are addressing energy challenges in homes, where 40% of all energy is used. Civic Insights, a private sector company, designed a new way to visualize the City of Palo Alto's permit process to make it easier and more transparent for applicants. Standby Taskforce, an NGO was created by Patrick Meier to combat violence. Anyone in Kenya with access to a cell phone reported human rights violations via a text message.

These messages were mapped and updated in real time giving complete coverage of Kenya. By clustering the number of calls by location Standby Taskforce generated a "heat map" that showed areas of concentration with most reported violence. This innovation of heat mapping was used in Haiti when a devastating earthquake struck the island nation. A live map of human distress calls updated in real time, guided United States Marine Core teams for strategic deployment.

In Colorado, the app Adopt-a-Hydrant allows community members to take responsibility for clearing snow off specific hydrants in their neighborhoods. The work of just a few minutes by citizens proves to be vital in case of a fire. Aligning interests, motivations and values in these collaboration examples are the key to their successes, which in turn facilitate today's governance. All sectors participate for efficiency and effectiveness.

Mission driven high-tech non-profits have the networks to put this highly skilled and technically savvy workforce in touch with meaningful causes in an effort to solve complex civic problems. Public agencies need only provide access to their single largest asset, the data. More than any other asset, public agencies produce a wealth of data, which is public. This data can be used to design helpful applications, create predictive analytics, find patterns and otherwise add great value to the agencies that create it. This form of data both transparent and free has been termed Open Data Systems and is a function of a new movement coined Open Government. Open Data enables citizens to access collective knowledge and information to create new services, suggest new ideas and identify critical bugs in the infrastructure and services they receive. Such a concept has led to creative third-party solutions to complex problems that cities may neither have the means or ability to pursue given the state of their budgets, limited resources or technical capabilities.

In the hands of the right people, civic innovation is now possible with a notebook computer, an Internet connection and available public municipal data. Over are the days where both public with public and public with private partnerships are a virtue of proximity. Collaborative efforts between the sectors are now boundaryless. Collaborative governance with civic innovation at its core can scale quickly and on multiple levels. Not only can an idea develop and scale quickly but the number of innovations in one agency is only limited by the bandwidth of the public administrators orchestrating the innovation. This starts to challenge the traditional model of government from public administrators providing a service to that of governance where administrators become more of a manager, facilitator and enabler of many actors working together to provide and find solutions to real life public administration challenges.

Therefore, we entered an age where there is no limit on the number of actors and collaborators that can engage with a local agency. Rather than delivering solutions, governments act as the platform to enable various actors to deliver solutions. Innovation is limited only by the imagination of the developers and the public data available for use. We encountered these innovations in public administration across the globe.

In India, we came across a wonderful and capable public administrator who described a fascinating public service initiative, which she had implemented in the state of Karnataka. The law is known as the Karnataka Guarantee of Services to Citizens Act of 2011 or SAKALA, which provides a guarantee of services to citizens in the State of Karnataka within a stipulated time limit. Under the Act when a request for a state service is made, a citizen is given an acknowledgment receipt with a SAKALA number (equivalent to a tracking number). This ensures that the request is processed within the specified days.

With the help of the SAKALA number a citizen can monitor on line and real time the status of his or her application. A citizen can even SMS from a mobile phone. In case of delay, a citizen can appeal to the next level of management directly and, per the requirements of the Act, demand a "compensatory cost" at the rate of 20 rupees per day for the period of the delay subject to a maximum of 500 rupees per application, in aggregate from the designated offending government officer.

Today, 668 state services under 50 departments provide transparency, accountability, efficiency and results—most everything we know good governance to be. Interest and motivation based sectoral alignment allows the state of Karnataka deliver better public administration services or govern with the use of private sector innovations in technology. The impact of the SAKALA initiative was so effective that 96% of services were delivered ahead of time and 100% transparency in workflow and accountability for officials were achieved. Additionally, the program reduced human interface, which in turn reduced the number of follow-up visits on the application processes, saving valuable time and resources for both citizens and government officials.

Never have these sectors (public-private and NGO) been so interdependent and so predisposed to collaborate, creating unprecedented opportunities for intersectoral as well as intrasectoral negotiated relationships or collaborations. These collaborations deliver important government functions, public goods and infrastructures while addressing and solving socioeconomic problems.

Collaborative governance as a practice has many different definitions and usages. Our colleagues Chris Ansell and Alison Gash from the University of California at Berkley provide a useful working definition, "a governing arrangement where one or more public agencies among themselves or directly engaging non-state stakeholders in a collective decision-making process that is formal, consensus-oriented, and deliberative and that aims to make or implement public policy or manage public programs or assets." Other scholars expand this definition to include different private sector areas and not for profit organizations. The private sector, the public sector and the not-for-profit/non-governmental (NFP/CSO/NGO) sector complement each other with increasing complexity and contain high levels of foundational overlap. The distinctions between sectors are increasingly without difference.

In existing literature on collaborative governance, Ansell and Gash identify critical variables that influence whether successful collaboration can be achieved. These variables include the prior history of conflict or cooperation, the incentives for stakeholders to participate, power and resources imbalances, leadership and institutional design. Similarly, there are several factors within the collaborative process itself that are helpful, including face-to-face dialogue, trust building (social capital) and the development of commitment and shared understanding. Virtuous cycles of collaboration tend to develop when forums, networks or organizations focus on "small wins" that deepen trust, commitment, relationships and shared understanding. Trust and relationship are core principles that we discuss throughout this book, especially in the context of Newgotiation.

Groups practicing intersectoral collaboration work to redistribute power and control from a central authority to many vested actors who are individuals or organizations. This sharing of power leads to innovation, cooperation, coordination and partnership on a higher level than is possible in typical hierarchical or bureaucratic systems. These collaborations address issues as diverse as HIV/AIDS, labor standards, obesity, corruption, delivery of public services from education, water, planning, engineering, trash hauling, development and construction of public infrastructures.

Collaboration, however, requires more than just working together. There must be a common mission, commitment to shared resources, power, and talent with no single individual or organization's point of view dominating. Dominance undermines collaboration, while assessing success of the collaborative efforts on a regular and methodic basis can build trust, relationship and shared commitment. Success that we define as efficiency, quality, price and/or delivery, and building upon positive feedback loops and forward momentum, can be a powerful driving force. Finally, we describe collaborative governance as good governance, which is the purposeful interaction of these three plus sectors to effectively and efficiently advance communities large and small. While the defining features of good governance are not universal or one size fits all, several significant characteristics also observed by the United Nations and the World Bank for example include transparency, efficiency, effectiveness, participation, accountability and results.

We worked at the UN with our public policy students to study governance in Least Developed Countries (LDC). Examining over 200 collaborative projects sponsored by the UN, we found that high quality governance, characterized by stakeholder collaboration, effective communication, high levels of accountability and transparency, and strong human and institutional capacity is critical to improving human development indicators for vulnerable populations in LDCs. On the other hand, poor stakeholder collaboration, ineffective communication and information sharing systems, low levels of transparency and accountability, and weak human and institutional capacity have hindered progress towards sustainable development in many LDCs.

The literature supports these findings. Two recognized scholars in this field, Kania and Kramer, suggest that individual organizations operating in isolation typically do not have the capacity to create systemic change. Cross-sector partnerships have been initiated in response to this restraint and better address complex social problems. Osborne, another scholar, writes that these partnerships are viewed as "efficient and effective mechanisms for developing inclusive communities; providing public goods and services; meeting the needs of target populations; and implementing public policy." Because coordinated stakeholder collaboration is integral to the success of all partnerships, poor collaboration can hinder progress towards a shared goal. Poor stakeholder collaboration can occur at any point during the partnership and almost always leads to reduced outcomes. The same is true in negotiation outcomes when parties instead of high level of collaboration resort to high level of competition to create winners and losers. We discuss this in our later chapters in this book.

Based on our UN work and experience, effective communication and information sharing in governance are essential elements for collecting divergent resources, eliminating misunderstanding and establishing public support. It is also a key step of innovation transfer, which requires to match interests of one party with the offerings of another. We discuss a very similar process in our Newgotiation steps of value creation and value distribution in chapters 4 and 6. Lack of communication and information sharing discovered in public administration in LDCs impedes the flow of ideas, creates mistrust and disapproval, and hinders the establishment of public consensus. When addressing a public policy problem, both stages of policy formulation and policy implementation need throughout communication in order to get various stakeholders to recognize the problem, as well as agree on the implementation methods. Poor communication and limited shared information create obstacles for policy implementation, identifying shared solutions and engaging various stakeholders. The similarities here in governance and negotiation are again quite remarkable. Lack of communication and mistrust is sure to hinder any reasonable negotiation process, yielding poor outcomes.

Professor Rothstein writes, "accountability and transparency in the public sector is a cornerstone in ensuring economic and social stability." Distrust undermines the social contract between the people and those who govern and detracts from the process of poverty eradication in LDCs for example. High levels of accountability and transparency in public institutions make the private sector and civil society more willing to partner with them in the delivery of public services. Furthermore, openness and transparency in government encourages valuable civic input and participation in decision-making processes. Community ownership is the difference between "done-to" and "done in collaboration with" and essential for instigating political will where it does not exist organically from the top down. Given that collaboration is a voluntary act, it is critical to understand the motivations and intentions of the sectors to forge the necessary bonds to act in collaboration. The concept in Newgotiation is no different. Understanding the motivations and intentions of the other party is crucial to the creation of value to distribute value and cut a deal.

We briefly examine here each sector, identifying challenges and looking for opportunities to collaborate. We seek collaboration to promote better public administration and more importantly to encourage "governance" today and tomorrow. The global financial crises, constrictions of markets, formation of complex networks, competition, growing fears of unemployment and huge infrastructure deficits present significant challenges for the public, private and not-for-profit sectors today. On the other hand, such significant challenges represent opportunities to collaborate through effective negotiation methods and skills to forge win/win opportunities of greater proportions for these three sectors. These challenges are mitigated by the evolution of the public sector through decentralization and the use of non-profit or for-profit contractors to perform service tasks associated with a particular skill and public administration. As our readers will note throughout this book, we borrow extensively from this literature of collaboration and collaborative governance to create value and distribute value in our Newgotiation paradigm.

We further suggest that Public Administration Professionals focus on public administration through collaboration, creating value for their organization and constituents while distributing value to various stakeholders and negotiating partners. Any framework for public administration must take into account the skills and capabilities needed for individuals and groups to act and how those skills meet emerging circumstances.

Today more than ever, we need our Public Administration Professionals to master the art and science of negotiation to avoid polarization and to forge collaborations between sectors to deliver effective governance. Seeking the public interest requires a willingness to become informed, to listen empathetically to various viewpoints, to collaborate, to network, to share, to build relationships and to take responsibility for not only ourselves, but more importantly for our constituents. This brand of leadership is still practiced for the most part at local levels of government as opposed to more politically motivated and ideologically positioned organizations in state and federal governments.

The evolutionary continuum in public administration views citizens as constituents, voters, customers, owners, partners and agents for change. The same evolution considers public administrators as public servants, trustees, managers, partners, facilitators and leaders. The main challenge is to create norms and common best practices among all these actors to advance society. The challenge is to create a new public administration not just in a hierarchical silo but open to service with standards of legitimacy, transparency, and efficiency across sectors. Frank wrote about such a model in an article he co-authored with a doctoral student of his entitled "From contract cities to mass collaborative governance" published in American City and County. In the article, the authors review the Lakewood Plan of 1954, which gave birth to the contracting model for municipal services across sectors using collaboration to deliver efficient municipal services.

From collaborative governance and all the negotiation pathologies and challenges, we examined, practiced and taught, we found a clear, practical and innovative but superior negotiation technique or mindset, which we call Newgotiation. We conclude and discuss in this book that Newgotiation is rooted in sharing and collaborating. Newgotiation has biological and cognitive science components along with a clear process that is impactful in the outcomes we seek in governance.

Among the thousands of trainees and students we had in our classes and seminars around the world, almost 100% say that they desire a win/win approach to negotiation because it leads to more pleasant results. However, in practice only 20% truly achieve the mutual gains approach. The remaining 80% select a more competitive practice of negotiation rooted in hard power. Max Bazerman wrote a brilliant book about the rationality of negotiators, and why they achieve win/loose results more often than win/win. There is quite a bit of literature on the topic of consensus building, books like "Getting to Yes" by Roger Fisher, where for example Fisher points out that in practice, most negotiators see negotiation as a competitive arm wrestling match in which 70% result in an impasse (0-0) and the remaining 30% with scores of (1-0), (1-1) (2-1). Only an elite group of Newgotiators see the possibility of scores in line with higher winning ratios of (10-10), (9-8) or (9-9). Only collaboration yields the latter results.

In this book, we focus on these public Newgotiators in order to:

a) Improve the PROBABILITY to close a better deal,

b) Improve the public VALUE of a deal by inventing and good decision making,

c) Improve the PRODUCTIVITY (higher winning ratio) to close a deal by sharing,

d) Improve negotiation with social networks for sustainability,

e) Improve deal making by recognizing and preventing conflict, and

f) Improve the rules and the language of negotiation in the context of collaboration.

However, it must be said at the outset that it would be naïve to believe that everything can be resolved by Newgotiating. Newgotiation is not about being nice, cooperative or submissive all the time, nor is it about being aggressive, assertive or competitive all the time. It is about all of those things balanced. It is about setting limits, being cooperative and competitive, it is about being empathetic, soft and gentle with people but tough in the defense of core values and interests. It is about creativity to find solutions to perceived problems that prevent agreement. After inventing the mutual gains approach with Lawrence Susskind, Robert Mnookin wrote a great book called "Bargaining with the Devil, when to negotiate and when to fight." In our book about Newgotiation, we discuss what is negotiable and what is not. More importantly, we discuss in this book a common language for all, which we call the "4-10-10 technique."

We hope that more will use the technique to achieve better results in public or private negotiations. The technique at a minimum is a comprehensive checklist for all that is necessary to negotiate effectively. Finally, Newgotiation is all about the frame. We discuss this concept of the frame throughout this book. While we cannot guarantee any negotiation results, we are confident that after reading this book you will be able to identify the wrong or the competitive frame (win/lose), to skillfully replace it with a more collaborative (win/win) frame aimed at mutual benefits.

KNOWLEDGE CHECK*:

*The detailed answers to all "Knowledge Check" inquiries and more can be found in Appendix A, in no particular order.

Creating value in newgotiation requires:

A. Seeing the other more than just a customer, but a partner and agent for change.
B. Making the customer king.

C. Yielding to customers' wants and desires.

D. Creating the best price as it is the only thing that matters.

Our newgotiation technique:

A. Promotes talking about price first then inventing options.

B. Invents one single option most useful to the most powerful negotiator.

C. Is always about being nice and never walk away from a deal.

D. Improves the public value of a deal by inventing and good decision making.

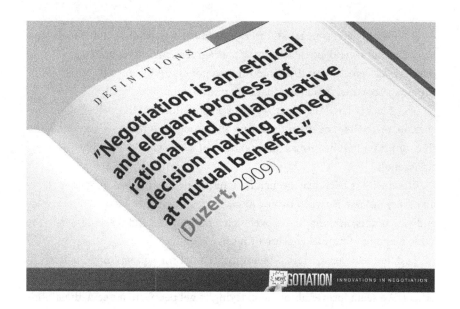

"Negotiation is an ethical and elegant process of rational and collaborative decision making aimed at mutual benefits." (Duzert, 2009)

DEFINITIONS

GOTIATION INNOVATIONS IN NEGOTIATION

CHAPTER 2:
GENESIS AND EVOLUTION OF NEGOTIATION AS AN ETHICAL PROCESS

The word "negotiation" finds its roots in Latin "neg" meaning to deny and "otium" meaning leisure. The English called this being busy, occupied or doing business. Not surprisingly the word "business" in Latin is "negocio." Time and evolution, managing feelings and emotions, matching desires and necessities, along with the game of power or the search for common ground, shape the modern art and science of negotiation. In more recent times, various scholars and practitioners have studied and defined negotiation in legal, psychological and business or economic terms.

Fisher, Ury and Patton define negotiations as "back and forth communication designed to reach an agreement" or "communication process with joint decision-making objectives." Similarly, Rubin and Brown define negotiations as "two or more parties attempt[ing] to settle what each should give and take." Carnevale and Lawler claim that Negotiation is a "form of symbolic communication that involves two or more people attempting to reach agreement on issues where there are perceived differences of interest."

Rubinstein defines negotiation as "a situation in which two individuals have before them several possible contractual agreements. Both have interests in reaching agreement, but their interests are not entirely identical. What will be the agreed contract, assuming that both parties behave rationally?"

The Black's Law Dictionary defines negotiation as "the deliberation, discussion, or conference upon the terms of a proposal agreement; the act of settling or arranging the terms and conditions of a bar-gain, sale or other business transaction."

The Business Dictionary generally refers to negotiation as "bargaining (give and take) process between two or more parties (each with its own aims, needs and viewpoints) seeking to discover a common ground and reach agreement to settle a matter of mutual concern or resolve a conflict."

Last but not least, Herb Cohen an accomplished practitioner said about negotiation "Life is a constant series of actions where we attempt to influence others. We seem forever absorbed in trying to get people to agree with us." This is where vocal expression plays a role in our training as negotiators. And "above all, negotiation is a pervasive process in which people ultimately attempt to reach joint decision on matters of common concern in situations in which there is initial disagreement. Thus, a negotiation always requires both shared interests and issues of conflict. Obviously, without commonality there is no reason to achieve resolution. So, without discord there is nothing to negotiate about."

With the backdrop of these diverse definitions highlighting and focusing on conflict, we, however, define our paradigm of Newgotiation for Public Administration Professionals as "an ethical and elegant process of rational and collaborative decision making aimed at mutual benefits." Our definition promotes relationship and trust, which we discuss in later chapters. Relationship and trust are two critical pieces of currency that every Public Administration Professional must possess to remain productive. As we discuss throughout the book, our Newgotiation paradigm is about a collective learning and decision-making process to score a win/win.

Negotiation as a primitive concept rises from the conflict, or the tension that we sense from seduction, rivalry and honor, from jealousy and the sense of competition to win and the envy to "destroy" our opponents. Challenging another man to a duel was not only considered a pinnacle of honor, but was a practice reserved for gentlemen. Dueling began in ancient Europe as a form of "justice" in which two disputants battled it out; whoever lost was assumed to be wrong. The first American duel took place in 1621 at Plymouth Rock. While with the inventions of rules in society we improved on the types of conflicts and the levels of violence associated with them, we continue to experience the biological and cognitive reactions associated with the brain. We are still human after all.

The primitive and instinctive nature of a negotiation comes from the limbic brain. This is the part of the brain that our prehistoric ancestors developed before the neo-cortex. The neo-cortex is the analytic brain, which developed with vocal expression or language. The limbic brain is part of the brain that does not speak, it feels, it is all about the five senses. Hence the value we place on aesthetics, which in Greek means sensation. This is why we dress well or smell good to impress our partners, relatives, friends, customers or constituents. In prehistoric times smell became a factor of attraction and therefore the basis for persuasion or conflict. In more modern times, perfume, drinking and dining and other enhancements were invented to precisely cause a chemical reaction in our limbic brain to please. Some cultures still value "wining and dining" as part of the negotiation process.

As the process of negotiation is set between various actors called negotiators, we now turn our attention to the anatomy, physiology and pedagogy of different types of negotiators in various contexts. In the process of discussing these topics we use perhaps dramatic examples, sometimes even exaggerated to make a point. We want to apologize at the outset for our examples, as we mean no harm or disrespect to any sector, anyone or any group.

We are big fans of each sector (public, private and not for profit) especially in the context of our argument about collaboration and collaborative governance. We appreciate their distinct motivations, intensions and interests because they provide us the opportunity to find elegant solutions to their problems during Newgotiations.

The private sector is wired to make money for its shareholders and there is certainly no shame in that. Fashioning non-monetary solutions to a conflict or a problem in the private sector will most likely not see that much interest. The public sector is appropriately wired to administer the rule of law, achieve social justice and deliver quality of life to its constituents, and there is certainly no shame in that.

Frank often says he is not elected to maximize monetary returns to his constituents in Rolling Hills Estates, but to keep them safe and deliver the quality of life they deserve and demand. While money is generally important for the implementation of desired policies in public administration, fashioning only monetary solutions to a problem in Rolling Hills Estates may not resolve the conflict. Finally, the not for profit sector is focused on its narrow mission, whether it is based on the space it occupies or the people it serves and there is clearly no shame in that. This being said, in today's collaborative world, citizens want more from each sector and those in leadership. While the challenges are great, the opportunities are suitable in this intersectoral space. We provide several examples in this book of models of collaborative governance and the application of our "Newgotiation" paradigm, which efficiently and dependably responds to the needs of this intersectoral space.

Before we discuss our paradigm, we want to focus on our definition and the ingredients in the definition to distinguish Newgotiation from conventional negotiations. We are committed to our definition of Newgotiation as "an elegant and ethical" process especially for Public Administration Professionals or officials. As our Newgotiation paradigm for Public Administration Professionals relies heavily on good governance skills, collaboration, building relationships and trust, we briefly discuss ethics and conflicts of interest to draw attention to these basic principles.

The improvements to ethical regulation of public service through the development of ethical policies, and the incorporation of the same into organizational and administrative cultures at all levels and branches of government, is highly supported by good governance literature and practice in public administration. In turn, the same literature supports the well-established practice that effective and efficient forms of governance improve the public's trust toward public officials and the government they serve. As we discuss in later chapters, "relationship" and "trust," of course, are the main ingredient of any win/win negotiation outcome for our Public Administration Professionals.

Public service forges a special bond between public servants and citizens. This special connection requires public officials of all levels and employees working for the public sector to place allegiance to citizens, laws, regulations and ethical principles above self-interest. Strict adherence to the rule of law and ethical principles are paramount to safeguarding the public's trust in government. Whether elected, appointed or hired, public servants must comprehend and practice ethical norms to attain good governance and eliminate improprieties.

In this chapter, we categorize ethics as a legal and reflective discipline used to resolve conflicts not only of technical means but also of societal means. Ethics is typically described as beginning where the law ends. Our moral conscience and developed values are the basis for the development of legal rules. Interestingly, ethics and law enjoy a symbiotic relationship for social good.

While each discipline has its own unique parameters, they overlap to advance society. This is also where elements of good governance such as transparency and accountability for example help protect the public interest.

Our colleague Terry Cooper in his book The Responsible Administrator reviews ethics as the study of moral conduct and moral status. He distinguishes ethics and morality by asserting that morality "assumes some accepted modes of behavior" by tradition, culture, religion, organization and family. He then suggests that ethics is "one step removed from action." In that "it involves the examination and analysis of the logic, values, beliefs and principals that are used to justify morality in its various forms." These values, beliefs and principles among other things include fairness and justice especially as they apply to the public interest in law and public service.

Although the overlap of the disciplines in law and public service and the relationship they enjoy is fundamentally important for the practitioners and their constituents, the laws of practice generally remain the indispensable discipline for sustained social good. Cooper refers to these laws as the "moral minimum." We agree. While they may be the minimum, these laws in practice however achieve more than just the minimum for the organizations and the constituents they serve. In this context, the establishment and enforcement of ethics standards, laws and regulations preserve the credibility and therefore the sustainability of the professional actor as well as the profession. In addition, these laws inspire a culture of trust and confidence in public servants and the governments or professions they serve.

We note, however, that not everything legal is ethical and in contrast not everything illegal is unethical. Recently the CEO of a prominent drug manufacturer raised the price of one pill used in the combat against HIV from $13.50 to $750. While the price hike was legal, the public outrage in what was perceived to be an unethical move brought public shame to the CEO and his company. The Birmingham March of 1963 was illegal under then existing Alabama law. Dr. King was arrested for defying an injunction that denied his and others right to march for civil rights under the United States Constitution. No one views this breach of the law as an unethical conduct. In fact, this march became the catalyst for the Civil Rights Act of 1964, advancing the United States in social justice.

The literature and practical evidence on ethics in public administration are quite complicated and multifaceted to suggest or recommend easy and simple solutions. Even the approach to public ethics varies from country to country taking into account historical, political and cultural context. Depending on this culture, some countries adhere to the strict rule of law and others resort to leadership skills to control corruption. In the United States, stricter and more comprehensive laws guide the concept of public ethics and conflicts. In northern European countries like Denmark, where self-interest is almost nonexistent according to Transparency International, stronger standards of integrity are cultural. In the United States, the rule of law both mandates and inspires ethical conduct, especially for medicine, law and public service. To illustrate our point, retired California Supreme Court Justice Ronald George once eloquently said about lawyers, "the title of professional requires that in daily practice, an attorney strive to transcend the demands of the moment to consider the greater good. Lawyers are not simply representatives or employees of their clients – they are officers of the court. That denomination reminds us that a lawyer's obligations flow not only to the client but to the courts and to the system of justice of which they are an integral part."

The rule of law exists to guide public servants in avoiding conflicts between the interest of the public and self-interest. Public laws and regulations establishing independent oversight over public officials and mandating public disclosures of private interests support informed and good decision-making, thereby improving public's trust and participation in the governance process. For example, California's experience in passing a comprehensive political reform package aimed at public ethics and conflicts of interest dates back to 1974.

In the aftermath of federal presidential scandal simply known in the United States as "Watergate" California became the first state in the union to pass a voter initiative known as Proposition 9 or The Political Reform Act of 1974 (the "Act"). The Act aims at strictly regulating political campaign activities, lobbyists and all public officials, state and local. The function of the Act is to obligate public servants to conduct the public's business in an orderly system of public administration. The Act codified in California statutes establishes unified rules of conduct for public officials. These rules are the public's minimum expectations from its public officials and are not open for good faith or even common-sense interpretation by the official. Therefore, among its most profound requirements, the Act requires public officials to disclose economic interests when they take office, annually while in office and when they leave office.

Conflicts arise when the responsibility of the public servant to one party interferes with the interest of another party. Black's Law dictionary defines conflict of interest as "a situation that can undermine a person due to self-interest and public interest." Merriam-Webster provides a more appropriate definition for our purpose, "a conflict between the private interests and the official respon-sibilities of a person in a position of trust." However, absent a law on point, having a conflict of interest is not, in and of itself, evidence of wrongdoing.

For many professionals, it is virtually impossible to avoid every conflict. The resolution of the conflict becomes a balancing act between fairness, transpar-ency and inspiration of trust. Frank as a mayor is required to live in his city of Rolling Hills Estates, California. He regularly votes on policy and expendi-tures fixing streets, pruning trees etc. One of those streets is the street he lives on. Presumably well-maintained streets improve property values, including his. Even though, technically, Frank may have a conflict voting on a street expen-diture, especially his own, based on his self-interest, his actions to maintain the streets of Rolling Hills Estates are fair, uniform and reasonable, and cer-tainly within the purview of his responsibility as an elected council member and mayor. No one will trust him less because of this conflict. So not every conflict is actionable conflict in the ethical context.

The best policy in the event of conflicts is to avoid it all together. Short of avoidance, few good habits such as prior disclosure and complete transparency may inspire trust and avert disaster. Public Administration Professionals are well advised to follow closely their organizational rules of ethics including seeking advice from professionals when in doubt. Finally, there is no substitute for good leadership. We discuss leadership and the value it brings to our Newgotiation paradigm in chapter 9.

KNOWLEDGE CHECK:

Newgotiation is all about selective influence.

A. True. Newgotiation is about targeting the opponent to lead him/her to the select decision.
B. False. Newgotiation is not about selective influence but a collective learning and decision-making process to score a win/win.
C. True. Newgotiation is all about making the other believe that you are right.
D. True. Newgotiation is the art and science of imposing your values.

The limbic brain is:

    A. Primitive and instinctive.
    B. Logical and linguistic.
    C. Not useful.
    D. Calculated.

The neo-cortex enables:

    A. Smell and touch.
    B. Aesthetics.
    C. Drinking.
    D. Logic and Language.

Everything legal must be ethical.

    A. True. The law is the most important barometer.
    B. True. Ethics and law go hand in hand.
    C. False. Not everything legal is ethical and not everything ethical is necessarily legal.
    D. False. Ethics is more important than law.

The reptilian brain creates behaviors of:

    A. Envy, food, drink, obsession, having more than the other.
    B. Love and empathy.
    C. Caring about the other's well-being.
    D. Cowardice.

CHAPTER 3:
ACTORS: IDENTITY AND CHARACTERISTICS OF NEGOTIATORS

"There are two ways of being creative. One can sing and dance. Or one can create an environment in which singers and dancers flourish."

Warren Bennis

In this chapter, we describe the critical typology of our negotiating actors as they orient themselves toward negotiation in practice. While most of us have ingredients of each type, we typically find our natural and comfortable space to negotiate, framed by our overall personality and context. While gender plays a role in some instances as we note in this chapter, every actor we describe can be male or female in various scenarios. Generalizing or stereotyping makes no sense for our purpose. As we discuss here, some actor types are clearly more useful in cooperative negotiations and in some cases even ideal for what we describe as our Newgotiation. Others on the other hand, are assertive, distributive and positional. We are not clinical psychologist, but observing practitioners, who know and recognize the different actors to design strategies to Newgotiate or find the right frame.

The Authoritarian

The Authoritarian is a person who sees the art of war, the games of power as the source of contentment of his ego. It can be a momentous behavior or more routinely stable state of being which becomes more difficult to change as people live in the same state of mind. He is a difficult negotiator because he is predisposed to use all means to achieve his end. He is a warrior, competitive and jealous. He is envious of what is best and is prepared to violate rules of ethics and even rules of law to be better than others. He can be destructive. The testosterone he produces reinforces his aggressive behavior to win at the expense of others. He does not share and prefers the domination method to create value without ever desiring to distribute value.

The authoritarian fits best in a hierarchical system of governance. He threatens those who do not agree with him and rewards those who accept his ways and rules. He impresses with people and objects of authority, uniforms, cars and houses. He is self-centered, so he will sculpt his image, his body, everything that feeds his vanity and self-esteem. He is risk averse. He does not like changes or tolerate new ideas unless they are his. In short, the authoritarian uses power as a process to make a decision. The literature calls this "hard" power as opposed to "soft" or "smart" power, which is based on diplomacy, economic reality, humanitarian and cultural influences.

The Authoritarian loves drama. He is typically cynical and pessimistic. He is the one holding his wife's passport at the airport, paying all the bills, doing the banking and making all the important decisions at home. As we mentioned, gender is not necessarily controlling here, a woman can be an authoritarian in this context as much as a man. They both play hard in seduction, they are tough, they don't call back when called and they don't have any empathy for the feelings of others. These competitive negotiators do not give much importance to the value of relationships. They are always suspicious, they even harbor hostility towards their opponents. The authoritarian listens less but talks more. He is used to using tools of coercion, threat or deception. The Authoritarian must make the final offer to close a deal. As we further discuss later, he is certainly not a prototype for our Newgotiation paradigm especially in public service.

The language to attract the authoritarian is more often all about being light, non-confrontational, unattached, simple and uncommitted. The individual who speaks more than him will turn off the authoritarian. Therefore, skilled Newgotiators allow the authoritarian to speak while developing options and best alternatives, which we discuss in later chapters. The skilled Newgotiator finds ways of praising the authoritarian's ego and caressing his vanity while attempting to move him to a desired and more neutral ground for consensus building and to getting to an agreement based on a different frame. The Authoritarian always wants to make the decision or have the last word.

Authoritarians are position-based negotiators. Skilled Newgotiators look for interests, preferences and desires to facilitate a win/win agreement on the merits. In our early French education, we learned the story of Napoleon's ambassador Charles Maurice de Talleyrand-Périgord. Ambassador Talleyrand negotiated the survival of a historic bridge in Paris, which is still used and marveled today as one of the most beautiful and ornate bridges in the world. Today the bridge links Les Invalides, the site of Napoleon's tomb, on the Left Bank with the Champs-Élysées on the Right Bank in the center of Paris.

Talleyrand's task was to dissuade a very powerful authoritarian, the emperor of Prussia Alexander III, who occupied and controlled Paris as a territory. The Prussian Emperor felt that Parisians and the French people were not worthy and culturally unappreciative of his goodness. To punish them the emperor notified Napoleon that he would destroy the culturally and logistically important bridge in the center of Paris. While the English ambassador Eaton obtained a short delay through his negotiations, the decision remained about the destruction of the bridge. The authoritarian was not moved.

The narrative or the frame about the negotiation had to change in order for France to save the bridge. Talleyrand knew that he had no chance to discuss this topic with this authoritarian, who had already made up his mind on his own terms. Talleyrand needed to change the narrative (as we often discuss in our courses "change the frame" from competitive, position based to collaborative, interest based) with creativity and by providing a graceful option to the emperor. When asked whether he had come on behalf of Napoleon to save the bridge from destruction, Talleyrand responded that he had come on behalf of the French people to invite his majesty Alexander III to come to Paris for the christening of this marvelous bridge as "Pont d'Alexander III." To this day Pont d'Alexander III remains a jewel of Paris.

Talleyrand's story illustrates textbook Newgotiation skills in defusing the authoritarian by creating a new, creative and graceful option or narrative or frame and standing out of the way of the authoritarian to allow him to make his decision, which he so desperately wants to make. In modern times, we know many of these authoritarians, who are trained in elite business schools to always win. The wisdom to deal with an authoritarian is to not enter in an escalation, or a symmetrical rivalry but to provide time and a "what if" with a smile. Mother Teresa used to say, "peace starts with a smile" and for a good reason especially in this context. Never underestimate the power of diplomacy and grace, even in hard negotiations.

The Controller

The controller is a negotiator who does not have power like the authoritarian but nevertheless loves to control the situation. He hates insecurity. He wants to have proof of love, respect and truth. The controller has a low self-esteem, but he has learned to express it through opposite characteristics. He is defensive and full of fear. He feels never good enough and terrified that opponents will sense this insecurity. The controller needs to be right and feel in control. Lack of control brings anxiety and fear forcing an aggressive response using the win/lose or the competitive frame. The controller is not able to concern himself with the needs and feelings of others because he must defend himself at all cost. He wants to use norms, legal framework and compliance as a source of trust.

The controller is not a dreamer. He is not a romantic; hardly an entrepreneur. He wants to have data, metrics, targets and measures. He likes routines, organized practices and proof to leave no doubt. In order to seduce or become attractive to a controller, a good negotiator has to be down to earth, responsible, logical and committed. Responsibility, education and maturity are skills a controller prefers. To be trusted by a controller a negotiator must show that he is rooted in tradition, love of family and rule of law.

Controllers do not look for pleasant moments or good times, they look for insurers, significant bankers, providers and battle tested men and women. They look for references of character and work ethic. By nature, controllers look for purity, transparency and integrity, before they trust or open their hart. As they are cautious, they tend to be aggressive at first and cold with people they don't know. Controllers are slow in analysis and decision-making because they fear mistakes.

Rodin once said: "everything that is done with time, time respects it." Controllers need to feel that it is the right time, the right mood, the right opportunity before anything can happen. The vocabulary of the controller includes honor, sense of duty, integrity, sincerity, good faith, morality, patriotism, equality, compromise, practicality, rationality, objectivity and one step at a time. Standards, norms, law, tradition, timing and context to make the controller relax are key to any negotiation with a controller.

Patience is usually rewarded when negotiating with a controller. As any good fisherman will tell you, there is no point trying to fish for trout at noon, the optimal times are early in the morning or after 6p.m. Similarly, a good negotiator must find the right time and opportunity to score a win with a controller. Negotiation with a controller is a game of endurance, a game of perseverance and adaptability to wait for the right time and context using the vocabulary that he is most comfortable with. We discuss negotiation context and timing in later chapters as part of our Newgotiation technique.

While we are compelled to understand and properly deal with authoritarians and controllers in real life negotiations, their typologies are not that useful for our Newgotiation paradigm without some adjustments or a new frame. The use of time, data, patience, creativity, elegance and relationships can address the need for the authoritarian to make the final offer or relax the controller to trust and enter our collaborative frame for Newgotiation.

As much as it is important to know how to change the narrative for an authoritarian to force a decision, he is pre-disposed to make, it is important to create conditions for controllers to be developers. Obeying rules, keeping with tradition while attractive on the surface, leave very little room for trusted creativity and innovation. Through timely patience and strong data on the facts, good negotiators allow controllers to develop their own narrative consistent with a more collaborative frame.

For example, a controller could never see success in a company such as Richard Branson's Virgin. Branson said time and time again that more than any other element; happiness is the secret to Virgin's success. While it is important to give value to data, to metrics and to risk prevention, it is more important in negotiation to teach controllers how to be more open, flexible, trusting and more focused on making other people happy; the basic requirements of the win/win or collaborative frame.

As we enter the era of more transparency especially in government circles, the challenge is to appreciate the genius of controller's dedication to the rule of law and risk aversion while making him trust more for the good of the whole. It is important to forge a relationship, create a way of life of trust, a culture of trust integrating precaution and risk management. That is precisely what IBM discovered in 2003, by surveying its 319,000 employees in a "values jam." The most common IBM values in the survey were "Trust and personal responsibility in all relationships".

We know that controllers are slow to trust. We previously observed that they are cautious and slow to act in an effort to protect themselves and their reputation. Sadly, this behavior reduces the likelihood of closing a deal as lack of trust is said to increase transaction costs while decreasing production. Kenneth Arrow, a Nobel Laureate in economics in partnership with various scholars from FGV, Stanford, MIT and Harvard, published a book in Brazil clearly articulating that most of the economic delay or economic bureaucracy in the world can be explained or attributed to the lack of mutual trust.

Based on our experience we extrapolate that the same is true in politics, negotiation and public administration. Social capital in the creation of human capital and trust are important topics that scholars and practitioners have tackled for centuries to improve economic, political, administrative and overall human behaviors and outcomes. We discuss them in the context of Newgotiation in later chapters of this book.

The Facilitator

The facilitator, especially the public leader, is a humanist with intentions to help, gather and integrate. She trusts people, accepts differences and conciliate at work and at home. She accommodates cooperation, flexibility and finds harmony. She does not like hierarchical systems and prefers collaboration to competition. She likes openness and transparency. She is a leader who enjoys the team management style. She likes training people and strives to elevate people by appreciating loyalty.

The facilitator is stimulated by the intellectual challenge, the conversation and learning. She enjoys the pleasure of the debate; she likes to challenge ideas and but does not mind changing her own views. She does not see disagreement as a source of conflict but an opportunity to revise and update beliefs, search for the truth in good faith without self-deception. Unlike the insecure controller and the self-centered authoritarian, the facilitator thinks and speaks, as "we" and not "I" or "me."

The facilitator is a giver. She does not have a strong ego, but a soft ego that credits others in the process. She is very effective, likes democratic decisions and sharing of responsibilities. She is a trainer who listens and identifies the strengths and weakness of her partners or teammates. She prefers long term to short term outlooks. She sees value in integration, kindness and diplomacy. She looks for peaceful relationships and avoids conflict. She does not seek or appreciate aggression but searches for cooperation and partnerships. She is empathetic, in terms of being able to walk in the "shoes of another" before making decisions.

The facilitator enjoys building consensus even in diversity or adversity. The facilitator mindset is all about social networks, integration, tactfulness and diplomacy. For example, the facilitator prefers to say, "Let's have dinner tonight. I can come to pick you up" as opposed to the authoritarian who is predisposed to say, "I am having dinner tonight. I want to invite you" and the insecure controller is programmed to say, "what about dinner tonight? Do you have other plans?"

Teaching our paradigm of Newgotiation is about understanding the biology of the human brain and also culture of mentalities of kindness aligned with the facilitator. More studies show that a child reared with love, care and gentleness is more intelligent and flexible therefore more prone to be a facilitator.

While it is not our purpose to prefer one gender to the other, women are biologically advantaged in this category. In a study published by Proceedings of National Academy of Sciences, researchers from the University of Pennsylvania School of Medicine found that men's brains are built "straight as an arrow highway" from the back of each hemisphere, where information is gathered, to the front, which controls the resulting behavior.

The neuropathways or the highways in "women's brains have more connectivity between the left hemisphere, which is more analytical, and the right hemisphere, which is more intuitive and can read social situations with far more complexity." While men exhibit some connectivity, it is much less profound. So, men "see and then do" while women are "more intuitive and collaborative." Finally, a similar study found that while men focus better on a singular task, women multitask better than men.

The Harvard Business Review reports on a recent study lead by Mario Daniele Amore of Bocconi University in Milan that overall, the more women on the board of a female-led firm, the more profitable it is likely to be. This study of thousands of family-owned business in Italy found that the presence of women improved cooperation, facilitating information exchange for ultimate success.

At the organizational level, the Harvard Business Review found that the most profitable companies are the ones with a culture of facilitation, care and empathy. Zeynep Ton, an associate professor at MIT and the author of "The Good Jobs Strategy" drawing on more than a decade of research concludes that operational excellence enables companies to offer low prices to customers while ensuring good jobs for their employees delivering superior results for their shareholders.

Sol Price, who revolutionized the retail market place with Fed Mart, Price Club and then Costco, invented this culture. At Costco 98% of store managers are promoted from within. Not surprisingly the care and empathy shown by management is reciprocated by very low employee turnover. More knowledgeable employees are more productive and innovative which reflects positively on the business and sales.

We contend that the facilitator trained to exercise care and empathy is the better Newgotiator. We are not surprised to see "corporate diplomacy" featuring facilitation, offered as part of the core curriculum in business schools today nor is it surprising to see "intersectoral leadership" highlighting collaborative governance as a core course in public policy schools. More and more law schools are offering strong curricula on mediation pedagogy focusing on the role of the facilitator and problem solver.

We learned that facilitators do not judge or assess like controllers. They are not predisposed to blame or punish like authoritarians but prefer thinking in terms of coevolution and shared responsibility. Facilitators are forgiving, revising and updating. They are neutrals, mediators, researchers and empathetic listeners, learners who accept diversity and tolerate divergence of opinions. They are more about the "how" than the "why" or even the "what".

During his postdoctoral work at Harvard, Yann met Arthur Levitt Jr., the longest serving chairman of the board of the Securities and Exchange Commission, who was on a book tour. Before Madoff and subprime scandals, Chairman Levitt and Warren Buffet predicted the risk of not creating mechanisms of control, parameters and standards of transparency to gain the trust of investors.

Chairman Levitt in a personal conversation also offered his views on the role of the invaluable CEO facilitator in the 21st Century by observing that in the 80's the CEO or the leader of an organization was typically a financial person because there were a lot of mergers and acquisitions and therefore cost reduction was a strategic priority for the leader. In the 90's the CEO was typically a lawyer because class action lawsuits and influencing key legislation were part of any corporate strategic plan. For example, the CEO of then AOL once said, "having influence on law creation is more important than technology." The CEO of L'Oréal in Brazil admitted that selling more than 180 million of bottles of shampoo products was good, but that L'Oréal really made money by favorably using Brazilian tax laws. Finally, chairman Levitt predicted then that the 21st Century CEO would be a diplomat, a facilitator, who will gather people from various sectors under the umbrella of collaboration and govern graciously. He was spot on again.

Indeed, authoritarian and controlling management styles are today quite archaic and inefficient. Facilitators have gained competitive advantage over more rigid authoritarian and controlling styles even in historically hierarchical organization.

We asked several generals and commanders in the military and police organizations in Brazil and the United States about their leadership style. What they described surprised us a little because we expected much more of an authoritarian style management on top of the organizational pyramid. They pointed out to us that we were thinking of conventional military or paramilitary structures and that there is nothing conventional about the administration of today's military or the law enforcement organizations in our cities or states. They described a flattened and horizontal organization with many technical and interdisciplinary facets to be nimble, innovative and efficient. Most importantly they viewed their role as facilitators of these interconnectedness that makes their organizations more complex but yet manageable.

We both teach in these organizational settings. The notion of community policing for example is all about empowering facilitators at every rank to positively engage the community and effectively provide for its security. Interdisciplinary collaboration and facilitation among the various branches of the military as well as their suppliers and contractors, makes for a more effective and efficient military. Similarly, bench officers or judges in the 21st century learn that a more facilitative role at the outset of any litigation promotes more settlements, saving enormous amounts of trial time and taxpayer money.

In our research for this book we also came across several examples of negotiators who are exemplary facilitators. These are leaders who understand the value of each sector under the umbrella of collaboration to govern and more importantly understand that modern governance is a triangle between meritocracies of experts and technocrats, elected executive representatives and participatory consultants.

Yann was called on to work with former President Lula's administration in Brazil to facilitate negotiations in tax, pension and labor reform policies. President Lula had selected 60 counselors from NGO's, Trade Unions, CEO's of Private organizations, Academics, Religious Leaders and Professional Organizations. This culture of participatory integration with public, private and not profits or more neutral experts was a very interesting application of modern governance by a natural facilitator.

Brazilian papers often proclaimed then, "70% of Brazilians believe in Jesus and 80% believe in Lula." Quite a remarkable statistic and statement given than most current world leaders are challenged with popularity ratings well below 50%. So, what can other world leaders learn from Lula's success in popularity at the time of his presidency? Rogerio Santa, CEO of Telebras, the broad band provider of the Brazilian government and participant to the council of 60 said it best; while "there were quite a few diverging views, differences of opinions and even egos in the room," Lula would never stop the debate, in fact as an extraordinary facilitator he encouraged more discussions among the group before coming back two weeks later to see if consensus could emerge for him to act as a chief executive of his country.

Lula understood as a former trade unionist the value of collective intelligence, encouraging the autonomy of the people to create their own arrangements and to promote collaboration and teamwork. Extraordinary facilitators like Lula see diversity as opportunities to revise and update even established beliefs to solve emerging or existing problems. Facilitators build capacity through coexistence and by collaborative learning. They learn by doing, experimenting and sharing resources to accelerate learning.

Today it is not about imposing or ordering a result by sheer power or control but about creating support and a platform for this exchange of ideas to occur stimulating the collective intelligence. Most leaders who fail in this endeavor are the ones who focus on one sector or one segment of several sectors while blaming others for all shortcomings. Our paradigm of Newgotiation benefits from the full spectrum of collaboration by all sectors to be more efficient and productive in any sector but more importantly in the representation of the public that we in public office are called to serve.

Last but not least, we want to touch on the facilitator's role within the local context and culture. The importance of speaking several languages practically and figuratively cannot be understated for a facilitator to be successful. The skilled facilitator not only speaks his local language but also is fully immersed in his local culture. He can tell the story of his city, town or village. His closeness to his community makes him the best agent for change and best facilitator in our new paradigm of Newgotiation.

For example, no one better than the mayor and his colleagues on the city council of Rolling Hills Estates in California to know the pulse of this semi-rural community where horses and peacocks co-exist; Where real cowboys still live in the western United States. Frank teaches around the world a topic near and dear to his heart: local governance and facilitative leadership. He is the first one to admit that while what he has to share is the best available scholarship and practice with a wide range of applications, it may or may not be suitable for consumption in another community, city, state in the United States or another country. It is up to the local facilitator to transfer or adapt suitable public administration and governance innovations or figuratively speak the language of his community. One size fit all is not the norm in public administration or in our Newgotiation. The local context and culture are undeniably important.

James Salacuse wrote an important paper articulating ten ways that culture impact negotiations. The lessons here are about doing as "the Romans do" in Rome. His research outlines 10 negotiation factors and compares them with respect to impacts. Only the local agent can facilitate effectively this negotiation process. The proverbial "faux pas," aggressive behavior or passive behavior, the unacceptable body language or simply words may dramatically impact the outcome of negotiations. Our advice is to always find a "Roman" to facilitate in Rome.

Figure 3.1: How culture impacts negotiation (Salacuse 2006).

The Entrepreneur

The Entrepreneur is risk prone and prefers the chance of a jackpot. He wants to be the first at everything as that is where he can make more money or create more opportunity. Like the venture capitalist from Silicon Valley or the trader on Wall Street, he is an optimist who is willing to overlook the chances of loss if he is able to envision the chances of great gain. He is driven by passion, by "the dream," and by the challenge to create something new.

Richard Branson in his book "Acredite em você e vai em frente" (believe in yourself and adance) published in Brazil said that when hiring people, he looks for someone with sparkles in the eyes, someone who will sweat for the company capturing the dream and someone who will passionately love what he does. The entrepreneur is dynamic, motivated, with a contagious enthusiasm. It is not surprising that enthusiasm in Greek means having "God inside." The

Entrepreneur likes distinctions. He wants to break rules, live closer to the edge, live like a revolutionary. He wants to be the first to read, the first to have, the first to teach. He wants to be the scout, the pioneer, the industry leader and the creator.

The Entrepreneur thinks mid-term and long-term investments create a new track record. He is the modern negotiator with the best and newest technology and the newest fashion. He is the champion of the newest pioneering and at times even dangerous lifestyle. Richard Branson's world tour in a balloon demonstrates this urge. His seduction to suborbital tourism is quite instructive of the mindset of the entrepreneur. He considers the financial reward and risk, but not before his enchantment by the concept, the challenge, the danger and the passion of human adventure. The thrill to achieve builds his enthusiasm, motivation, creativity and innovation. The founders of YouTube and Myspace told a group of Brazilian entrepreneurs the need to focus on these skills to mimic the culture of the Silicon Valley in Brazil. The need to motivate agents of change to create, invent and be thrilled in the process.

Years after the success of bringing Elite Modeling Agency to Brazil, Ricardo Bellino, a self-made entrepreneur, created a new interest, a dream and adventure to uplift the Brazilian lifestyle. Bringing internationally recognized luxury to Brazil meant seducing another entrepreneur already in the business of providing for the rich and famous elsewhere. Despite being turned down by Donald Trump for Trump Towers and Jack Nicklaus designed Trump Golf Resorts, Bellino persevered determined to persuade Trump.

Recognizing Trump's complex skills as a negotiator and his entrepreneurial spirit, Bellino delivered to Trump compelling and mostly exciting data about the Brazilian lifestyle. He was creative but on point. He told Trump that the world's second largest fleet of private helicopters and jets reside in Brazil. He told Trump that Rua Oscar Freire, a street in Sao Paulo, is the 8th most luxurious street in the world and only second in the Americas to 5th Avenue in Trump's hometown of New York. He also pointed out that Brazil is the largest economy in Latin America with a purchasing power parity of $1.04 trillion and a real growth rate of 3% annually.

All this optimism and excitement transformed Trump's cynicism into dynamism and enthusiasm. Bellino had succeeded to motivate this successful agent of change to be thrilled to bring his brand to Brazil. Interestingly, Bellino then switched roles from an entrepreneur to a facilitator, a more suitable role to negotiate the implementation of the dream between Brazilian investors and

Trump. This switch is not uncommon in our context for Public Administration Professionals, especially when we as mayors and council members tout the dream of our communities to agents of change in terms of economic development and later become facilitators to implement the development. Entrepreneurs first create the optimism and excitement necessary to bring the change, and facilitators later implement the change among community organizations, citizens and various stakeholders.

The Visionary

The visionary thinks about time, about legacy, about how he will be remembered. Is he a symbol of generosity, integrity, justice, or moral elegance? Generally, he is prepared to sacrifice himself for a greater cause and for future generations. He thinks long term. He thinks of peace, progress and prosperity of his community, and even of his fellow men. His ultimate legacy and purpose in life is what drives him.

The visionary is not interested in short relationships but in sustainable and long-term relationships. He does not seek immediate satisfaction. He is a social planner; he works with societal challenges, a conflict in a family perhaps. He likes solving problems. He does not fear adversity because he is always after the solution. The visionary makes a great social assistant, a nurse, a mathematician, a historian, potentially a mayor, a governor or president on a good day. But he is also a dangerous extremist.

The visionary is even more risk-prone than the entrepreneur; he is prepared to take drastic measures for the good of many. He is philanthropic. He is for causes grander than himself. He is prepared to say "no" based on principle if that principle serves his cause. He is an idealist who can do a lot of good or be dangerous. The ends may justify any means for the visionary. While the pertinent question in negotiation may be "when" for the authoritarian, "what" for the controller and "how" for the facilitator, it is mostly "why" for the Entrepreneur and the Visionary. The cross over here to leadership literature is quite remarkable. We discuss leadership, the importance of mission, vision and goals in chapter 9.

About 10 years ago during one of his seminars to Brazilian judges Yann asked an interesting question: If an Extra Terrestrial were to land on Earth in peace and ask for 5 ambassadors of mankind, who would you suggest? In that context, Mandela, Martin Luther King, Gandhi and Mother Teresa" came up regularly.

Naturally no billionaires, athletes or pop stars were mentioned. Although given that this was Brazil the football/soccer star Pele came up few times. The nominees were people, who made a disproportionate sacrifice to change the world for the better without any particular authority but with a very strong vision for the future.

What was more surprising however, Yann then asked the same question in China, India, France, Colombia, United States, Portugal and Nigeria to more than 20,000 professionals; with few exceptions, the same four always came up. This is because we as human beings are preconditioned to love visionaries. The attractiveness of people with a "think different" mindset has been with us for centuries. In his book "Negotiating with the Devil, when to Fight and When to Negotiate," Robert Mnookin observes that people who resist against dictators or dictatorial regimes and choose not to make concessions, typically have a greater sense of duty. When the standard was "Colonialism", Gandhi envisioned a change in this standard. Mandela chose to stay 27 years in prison rather than finding an easy arrangement with the dictatorial regime of Apartheid. As a visionary, he made the sacrifice for the long-term to realize a peaceful and harmonious society in South Africa.

The visionary thinks in terms of concession, criteria and moral standards—not social standards. He has a categorical imperative that makes him impervious to temptations. He prays, he isolates himself. He is prepared to renounce the immediate pleasure, which makes him so difficult to corrupt. Faithfulness, integrity, morality is what he seeks. Moral elegance and ethics drive his actions because it is his purpose—and his values. These same visionaries come up in our leadership literature and discussion. This is certainly not surprising to us.

Apple's success is attributable to this same "think different" notion. With images of Gandhi, Martin Luther King and Picasso in various advertisements, Apple made its case to its fans and customers. The vision of Steve Jobs has become synonymous with culture for all. The "why" is the ultimate motivation of any negotiation. Simon Sinek said start with the "why." The "why" represents the purpose, the dream, the lifestyle, the mood and the sensation. It is precisely where the limbic brain operates. The limbic brain is all about the implicit, the imagination, the holistic perception and the mindfulness. Francisco Varela called it the "embodied mind," all what we smell and sense, and the aesthetics. People and companies who are successful in our new paradigm of Newgotiation always start with the why, the purpose, the context, the culture and the atmosphere. The "what" and the "how" or the price and terms as secondary topics always follow later. In the context of political campaigns, we all remember the "why" in Bill Clinton's slogan "it is the economy stupid," Barak Obama's "hope and change," Emanuel Macron's "together France," Marine Le Pen's "chose France," and Donald Trump's "make America great again."

We also know that Apple and Harley Davidson consumers buy them for the "why" and certainly not for the price or terms. These iconic brands appeal to our limbic brain. They exemplify the visions of "changing the world" or the "American freedom." While Apple and Harley Davidson always start with the dream, context, long term, purpose and culture, the "how" and "what" are the logical part of Newgotiation addressing the needs of the neo cortex, which is the more developed part of the human brain. In other words, the neo cortex is involved in higher functions such as sensory perception, generation of motor commands, spatial reasoning, conscious thought and language.

The most valuable skill of the visionary public leader is precisely the flair, the intuition, the imagination, the culture and context of the moment to shape and eloquently describe the "why." This addresses the limbic brain before taking any discussion to the "what" or the "how" to involve the neo cortex. Political campaigns have been won and lost on the "why," arguably voters drawn to this message rather than the possibility of "how' and "what." We therefore follow this messaging framework in describing our Newgotiation paradigm and process.

KNOWLEDGE CHECK:

As a negotiator, the authoritarian:

    A. Listens more than s/he talks.
    B. Creates and makes concessions.
    C. Prefers domination to create value.
    D. Loves peace.

The controller:

    A. Is more risk prone than risk averse.
    B. Uses norms, standards, legal framework and compliance as a source of trust.
    C. Likes to brainstorm about new ideas.

D. Trusts people.

The facilitator, on the other hand:

A. Uses power tactics to lead groups.
B. Accommodates cooperation and finds harmony.
C. Uses time to pressure fast decisions.
D. Uses fear to make people cooperate.

The entrepreneur is likely to hire someone:

A. With sparkles in his/her eyes capturing the dream of the project or company.
B. With credentials supported by documentation, standards and benchmarks.
C. With a business plan detailed in a spreadsheet.
D. With established traditions.

CHAPTER 4:
NEWGOTIATION AS A PROCESS

"Be a yardstick of quality. Some people aren't used to an environment where excellence is expected."

Steve Jobs

There are four anatomical steps to anchor our Newgotiation technique. They are: preparation, value creation, value distribution and implementation. Our study of thousands of negotiations also demonstrates that there are 10 simple but most relevant elements that directly correlate to these four steps. These elements include context, interests, options, power, communication, relationship, concession, conformity, criteria and time. Therefore, in order to create a common language or a workable collective blueprint of Newgotiation, we discuss below our four steps and the application of each of the 10 elements to the four steps in every negotiation. Also, to assure success through implementation in each negotiation, we propose 10 benchmark criteria for implementation and evaluation of our Newgotiation paradigm for future use. We call this entire process the 4-10-10 Technique of Newgotiation. This logic model is for every negotiation especially for Public Administration Professionals. While the model is not a "magic bullet" to solve all conflicts, we recommend its methodic use to improve productivity, probability and value in all negotiations.

We see the profile of all Newgotiators as movable with education and training. Newgotiation is all about transformation. While controversy may be necessary to negotiate, facilitating a frank discussion accelerates the meeting of the minds and the collective good decision-making process. Jack Welch calls this "friendly frankness."

Before we get to the substantive content or the anatomy of our Newgotiation technique, some preliminary basics on process are key to the success of the outcome. First, accurately knowing the profiles of each participant to this Newgotiation is critical to our approach and preparation. We both say to our classes, preparation is vital. For example, is an elected official or a political appointee participating? Is there staff representation in the group? Are lawyers present? Are consultants facilitating? Are all stakeholders with authority or legitimacy there? After this preliminary step participant identification, recognizing the type of a negotiator is the next step for a skilled Newgotiator to lay down the strategy before approaching the negotiation table.

Good Negotiation is all about the frame. The key here is to avoid conflict between different types of actors such as an authoritarian, controller, facilitator, entrepreneur or a visionary. The priority is to strategize in framing the process in a collaborative frame (win/win) rather than a competitive frame (win/lose). Also, to think about what to do and who to call if the frame is in fact competitive. Sometime simply knowing when to walk away from a competitive frame to wait for a better collaborative frame is crucial. Here thinking about the appropriate social capital and human capital is beneficial to the process. The public leader or official must obtain this preliminary information before engaging in the process based on her preparation or ask her staff to procure this information before starting the negotiation.

Next is to build a relationship among the participants to explore the multiple approaches to transforming beliefs, perceptions, emotions and visions. It is all a pedagogical process of joint decision-making through various life skills such as empathetic listening, communication, ethics, passion, reconciling interests through collaboration and enthusiastic vision building or perhaps dreaming. Rushing to negotiate may have serious long lasting and disastrous consequences compared to taking time to build a relationship based on mutual respect and trust. We discuss these life skills throughout the book.

Finally, good decision making is fundamentally important to framing and implementing the negotiation process. To cover decision analysis as a method that determines the best decision even when there is conflict or uncertainty, we asked one of our colleagues to contribute the next chapter about "The Six Elements of Decisions Quality." Professor Abbas is a well published expert in decision analysis. He studies decision as a reflective and complex topic in individual and organizational environments. We note the importance and the high correlation of each element of good decision making in our Newgotiation process.

KNOWLEDGE CHECK:

Newgotiation can resolve every dispute:

A. True. As talking about price first then inventing options takes care of everything.
B. True. It is the best method known to mankind.
C. True. Being nice is always helpful.
D. False. Negotiation is not a "silver or magic bullet" does not solve all problems but certainly provides a common language and framework to work hard for better results.

A good newgotiator is:

A. Someone who is focused on a target and knows how to hit it.
B. Someone who listens and learns from the other to make an ethical, rational and collaborative decision.
C. Someone who is able to manipulate others.
D. Someone who always has the last word.

CHAPTER 5:
The Six Elements of Decision Quality

By Ali Abbas, Ph.D.

"A good decision is based on knowledge and not on numbers."

Plato

Decision analysis is a rigorous method that determines the best decision alternative even when there is uncertainty about the outcome. The rules of decision making apply to a single decision maker, but many important decisions need to be analyzed at an organizational level. This chapter explains the basic elements of a decision, along with reflections on the effects of organizational complexity and incentive structures on the decision-making environment.

The Six Elements of a Decision

If we asked a person at random in any fortune 500 company or government enterprise to rate the quality of people they work with, many will answer that they work with intelligent and highly-qualified individuals. If we asked them to rate the quality of the decisions made by their organizations, they will answer that the quality is low. Where does this discrepancy come from?

To begin, it is important to note that many people have not taken a course on decision making, and many have not even heard that this is a subject that is taught. Organizational leaders often acquire decision making skills in their area through years of practice in a particular field and then rely on intuition to make decisions. The notion is that the expertise that they have acquired (and the capital that they have built) is sufficient to provide them with the skills they need to make a good decision. As is well known, however, intuition is not always sufficient to make a decision particularly when there is uncertainty or when new situations arise.

The six elements of decision quality (Howard & Abbas) provide a mechanism to help us think about the various aspects of a decision. They can be used as a checklist and are often represented by a chain. Figure 5.1 illustrates the six elements of a decision in the form of a chain, where the strength of the chain is only as strong as its weakest link. Below is a description of the six elements; for more information, review Howard and Abbas (2015) in our bibliography.

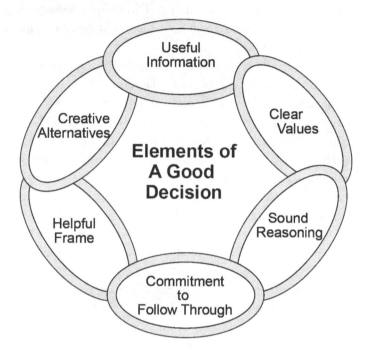

Figure 5.1: The six elements of a good decision.

The first element of decision quality is the decision maker (and the stakeholders that are affected by the decision). Failing to consider all people affected by the decision can result in several disputes after the decision is made. We discuss in this book the importance of stakeholders for our collaborative and right frame. Think of a decision involving the continued existence (or removal) of a hazardous oil refinery in the middle of a city. The refinery has been there for generations, but the city has now expanded, and homes are within much closer proximity. The decision must not come from a local government alone but instead must include the residents near the refinery, the employment of people affected by removing the refinery, the people affected by a possible change in oil process and many others. Quite often in organizational (or government) decision making, it is useful to pause and ask: who is the decision maker? People tend to forget to ask that basic question. If we omit a group of stakeholders, we must not be surprised later if we find resistance to the decision that has been made. When it relates to negotiations, it is almost impossible to reach an appropriate framework for negotiating when a set of stakeholders have been omitted. The first element also involves a commitment of the decision maker(s) to follow through. After all, if we have no intentions to follow through, then why are we analyzing the decision in the first place?

The second element of decision quality is the frame of the decision, which involves identifying the decision; identifying the different perspectives involved and determining the boundaries of the decision. This involves identifying "What is taken as given?", "What needs to be decided now?" and "What will be decided later?" Failing to identify the right frame is common and can lead to poor decisions as well as failed negotiations. Yann and Frank discuss the "frame" in terms of competition or collaboration throughout this book.

Consider for example a multi-stage decision about a person who is considering leaving work and going back to school. The decision he might pose is: I have received admittance for several graduate schools, which school should I go to after quitting work? Quite often this question is asked, and it implies that he has "taken as given" that he is leaving work. There are of course many other alternatives such as taking evening classes or enrolling in an online degree program while keeping his current job. If he has indeed made the decision to quit his job and go to graduate school, then the decision about which school to accept the offer from becomes appropriate. That decision might include many factors such as the location, the reputation of the school, tuition, the placement rates and the quality of instruction. These are the factors to help with the current decision: what should I decide now? Then there are decisions to decide later. For example, where will I live when I go to graduate school? Will I ride a bike, take transportation or buy a car? A decision is to be decided later if its alternatives do not affect the decisions made now.

In organizational settings, people are often given boundaries on their decisions, or requirements that they are asked to meet. For example, a project manager might be given a decision to decide whether to make minor improvements to an existing product or to make major changes. This decision already takes as given that the company will continue to manufacture that product. A good frame would challenge the boundaries to make sure they are set correctly or updated when new information arrives. Similarly, if a design engineer is given a set of requirements, such as designing an engine that does not exceed a certain weight, the engineer must check to see if exceeding the weight at the expense of a much better engine or lower cost might be suitable for the company.

The third element of decision quality is the proper identification of the feasible alternatives. Without a good set of alternatives, there is no decision to be made. If you have only one alternative, then you should just do it. Quite often though, there are many more alternatives present. The alternative that results from the analysis is very often one of the alternatives considered (or a hybrid of alternatives considered). If you have not selected an appropriate set of alternatives to analyze, then you are missing out on value from the very beginning regardless of the analysis that will follow.

The fourth element of decision quality involves identifying the preferences of the decision maker. This involves identifying appropriate interests, values and trade-offs among the different objectives. This element is also essential in negotiations. In their Newgotiation paradigm, Yann and Frank talk about interests, options and alternatives.

The fifth element is one that most enterprises spend a lot of time and money on: this is the information element that captures the information and uncertainties about the decision in a meaningful way. Decision analysis provides a method to quantify information and to determine the economic feasibility of gathering more information. Many organizations attempt to continue gathering information to minimize all uncertainty, but, indeed, gathering too much information (as companies often do) might not be the most prudent thing to do.

Finally, the sixth element of decision quality is one that is quite often underestimated in organizations and results in poor decision making despite the efforts conducted with each of the previous elements. This sixth element is the logic or the choice criterion by which the decision is made. The norms of rational decision making imply that the choice criterion is to choose the alternative with the highest expected utility (von Neumann & Morgenstern)

Opportunities and Challenges for Decision Making in Organizations

The implementation of decision analysis in an organization requires a change in culture that rewards individuals based on the quality of the decision instead of the outcome. Thinking in terms of this method can help resolve many issues we face in organizations today. Decision making in organizations involves having multiple individuals with different beliefs, objectives, incentives and preferences.

Within this structure, it is important to incorporate various pieces of decision quality from various individuals. Human resources, for example might be better positioned to forecast the salaries of future hires, marketing departments may better forecast demand for a product, while engineering departments might be better suited to forecast technical success.

Incentive structures also influence the decisions made at an organizational level. Incentives are present to decentralize the decision-making process and provide a mechanism for performance. However, they often have unintended consequences if not set appropriately. Suppose that a manager faces two projects that include conducting "minor upgrades" to an existing product, or a new innovative project with "major upgrades". The "major upgrades" project might have a higher expected value but might also have a higher probability of losses. A manager who is penalized by having losses (regardless of the quality of the decision) might select the "safer" alternative of "minor upgrades" even if it provides less value for the organization on the long run.

Sometimes various departments might have different incentives and objectives. An engineering department, for example, might wish to have less product recalls and so it might aim to delay the introduction of a product to market. A marketing department, on the other hand, might wish to gain market share and so it might push to introduce the product to market fast to gain market share and meet its incentives. Balancing these various objectives is achieved by identifying higher-level objectives of the organization and quantifying the uncertainties. For example, if the goal is to maximize the profit, then the organization must determine the expected utility of maximizing profit for each alternative.

Organizational decision making is often complicated because of the presence of various types of biases resulting from (i) cognitive biases and (ii) motivational biases due to objectives and incentives. Cognitive biases result from psychological biases by nature of being human. For example, anchoring is one such cognitive bias where individuals to give more weight to items that are in the salient memory. Motivational biases (as the name implies) result from different motivations such as different preferences and incentive structures. A good decision analyst will observe the presence of both cognitive and motivational biases and provide facilitation to ensure that the preferences of the stakeholders are represented. Many probability encoding techniques take into account cognitive biases and attempt to minimize their effects during belief elicitation.

Failing to use the correct logic is also very common in organizational decision making. Many enterprises think about the elements of decision quality and spend a lot of time and effort gathering data and information, but then use arbitrary choice criteria for making a decision. The crux of decision making lies in the idea that the quality of a decision does not rest on the outcome obtained, but on the quality of the analysis and thought.

Most arbitrary methods of decision making are motivated by three factors:

- Simplicity;

- Aversion to using probability to describe uncertainty; and

- Reluctance to assign explicit preferences and trade-offs in decision problems.

Simplicity is not an excuse for using a wrong decision criterion. Failing to incorporate uncertainty can result in making the wrong decision. The reluctance to assert preferences and then using an arbitrary choice criterion results not only in poor decision making, but also in absurd preferences and trade-offs. The role of the decision analyst is not to use an arbitrary method for simplicity but rather to help the decision makers incorporate the elements of decision quality in a meaningful way and observe the organizational complexities that need to be resolved to provide a healthy enterprise decision culture.

Ali once wrote, in OR/MS Today, "it is useful to think of decision-making as a calculator. The inputs to the calculator are the elements of decision quality: the alternatives, preferences, uncertainties, information, pros/cons and the bigger picture from the perspective of the decision-maker. The calculator itself is the logic that determines the best decision given the inputs you provide." Ultimately, people and not data make decisions.

CHAPTER 6:
THE 4-10-10 TECHNIQUE OF NEWGOTIATION

"If I had eight hours to chop down a tree, I'd spend six sharpening my axe."

Abraham Lincoln

We all are familiar with the old adage "preparation is everything" or the sports cliché that a football team on game day is as good as its last practice. Negotiations are won or lost before any substantive meetings between negotiators. Preparation and the quality of that preparation is key. Good preparation takes into account a well-designed process, meticulous stakeholder analysis and good decision making.

A stakeholder analysis is a framework to analyze stakeholders. This helps us understand behavior, intentions, interrelationships and interests of stakeholders in the negotiation. The analysis also helps us assess the influence and resources stakeholders bring to bear on decision-making or the implementation processes.

A good amount of negotiations or projects fail because we miss or misidentify a stakeholder. For example, ignoring the residents of a coastal community may be a fatal mistake for offshore drilling negotiations. Ignoring the equestrians in an equestrian community while attempting to build a golf course may be the demise of the project.

Good preparation through listening and collection of relevant data also postpones the moment of anchoring the critical event in the negotiation. Most negotiators fail because of lack of preparation and for anchoring the critical moment, mostly the price of the project or contract, too soon. Once the price is exposed, the Zone of Possible Agreement (ZOPA) becomes one price against the other or no deal. This is really the third step in our four-step process. Ignoring steps one and two can be fatal to any negotiation. Everything else to achieve the win/win become secondary or much more difficult to discuss and more importantly much more difficult to achieve. Reaching ZOPA prematurely bypasses two critical steps of our Newgotiation technique, namely preparation and value creation.

Value creation is the definition of the "why" for the Newgotiation by identifying interests, options and possibly alternatives to options. This is the moment to be creative, innovative and descriptive. Not surprising that entrepreneurs and visionaries love this step. The more creative the negotiator, the more options are created—and the more options that are created, the more possibilities for a deal. This is where empathetic listening matters. This is where every stakeholder counts. The more we explore "what if's" the more we propose solutions to problems. The value creation step is precisely to address or suspend criticism and invent options and then alternatives to solve problems.

In an organizational context for example, options to improve productivity, quality of product, organizational climate or culture are key to success. This is the step to build trust by brainstorming, asking and listening. This is the moment to build a joint dream or opportunity. Value creation is all about getting to "yes." H. Raiffa in his book "The Art and Science of Negotiation" emphasizes the importance of building trust, common purpose and belief. Most negotiators do not even agree about the hypothesis without this step let alone agree on the solution of the equation. The key is to expand the focus in the creation of coherence between the limbic brain and the neo-cortex. The value creation step (our second step) is the only way to achieve the desirable outcome by getting to "yes" with great velocity and value.

A small number of negotiations are distributive, or single-issue negotiations. A negotiation over a tractor, for example, may involve the single issue of price. These negotiations are really not our focus here. Far more commonly in the public sector, however, negotiations involve multiple issues. These negotiations are known as integrative negotiations, or value-creating negotiations, because they allow the negotiating parties to integrate various sources of value through creative exchanges.

We offer as a case study our negotiation of building a fire station for a California city. While we proposed a public private partnership through a methodology called lease lease back, our creativity and value creation did not stop there. The methodology helped the city finance a brand-new fire station with private funds through bonds. It also shifted construction and delivery risk to the private sector. But more importantly for the city, it allowed the city to take possession of a "turn key," all-inclusive fire station operations including fire trucks and engines as part of the deal. This creativity brought about an efficient and effective public private negotiation based on interests and values to serve those interests. The city was able to focus on good governance and public administration, while the private sector using its building and procurement strengths delivered a state-of-the-art fire station. We call this metaphorically negotiation about the whole of the pie as opposed to the sliver of the pie. A holistic discussion about various interests to maximize negotiation potential. This is why we claim that our Newgotiation process improves the public value of a deal by inventing and improves the probability of a better deal.

In the fire station negotiations, we asked ourselves how can we make the most of integrative negotiations, creating as much value as possible to then distribute among the private and public sectors? The negotiation literature about guidelines to create value tracks our practical experience in this case study.

Generally, when negotiators encounter differences with negotiating parties, as we did in this case study, they tend to view this as a roadblock. In fact, differences more often are "opportunities to create value in negotiation," write Harvard Business School professor Max H. Bazerman and University of California, Berkeley professor Don A. Moore in their book Judgment in Managerial Decision Making.

Negotiators often get stuck because they remain focused on one aspect of the deal or transaction. We broke that impasse by asking a lot of questions to identify all interests in our fire station case. We would not have been able to structure the deal if we did not know for example that city had specific tax revenues for 15 years. This knowledge helped us structure the term of the lease making ownership of the fire station by the city a reality at the end of those 15 years. If we had not asked what an ideal deal for a fire station looks like for the city, we would not have known about the necessity to procure fire trucks and engines as part of the deal.

Negotiators think methodic organization is key to resolving one issue at a time. That may be true in some instances. However, in integrative negotiations, especially in the public sector, the better approach is to discuss multiple issues explaining clearly that settlement occurs only when everything is discussed and agreed. In fact, negotiating one issue at a time prevents capitalizing on differences with trades across issues. Metaphorically, baking the whole of the pie or enlarging the size of the pie. Discussing or negotiating about the sliver of the pie will only yield the sliver.

Integrative negotiations don't require sacrifices in the name of cooperation. On the contrary, they allow negotiators to get more of what they want by identifying what each party values most. As we describe a "bigger pie" or "enlarging the size of the pie," where all parties benefit from the value creation process. Again, once metaphorically the pie is enlarged, there is more value to be claimed by all. Our fire station project made sense once we had identified all interests for all stakeholders (including time of deal, equipment etc.). Once the interests were identified and aligned with elegant options and solutions, we were prepared to distribute values.

Our third step in our four-step technique is value distribution. This is when we describe or justify the critical moment for the negotiation or the price. Having explored all interests, and invented all possible options without commitment, this is the time to expose and justify our decision or price with objective standards and based on evidence that we obtained during our preparation.

The moment of value distribution is when we transform the options of each interest into reciprocal concessions. This is the time we divide the equities or divide the "pie." The opportunity created by this step before getting to ZOPA cannot be understated. This step is also commonly known as the compromise.

Once the distribution of value is over, the fourth and last step is all about follow through or implementation of the agreement as negotiated. This step is also about compliance with law and sustainable future. Given the complexity and importance of the first three steps in our technique that we discuss above, the fourth step yields as good results as the quality of the first three. Last but not least, as much as preparation is key to any good negotiation, implementation is everything. If the negotiated agreement cannot be implemented, not much value can come even from the best of negotiations.

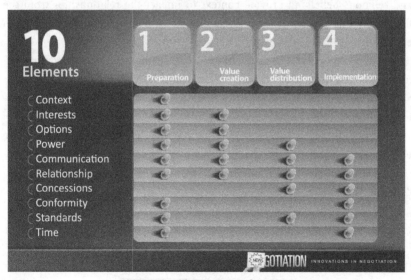

Figure 6.1: The 4-10-10 technique.

Next, in our 4-10-10 technique, we take our four steps through the 10 elements that we identified through our research and practice of all types of negotiations. These 10 elements play a substantial role in the outcome of the negotiation. Like stakeholder analysis, discussing each relevant element in detail during all four steps is key to the success of the technique. In our chart at the beginning of this chapter, we identify each relevant element vis a vis each step of our technique. Not surprisingly, the crucial preparation step bears relevance to most of our elements.

Context

The first element "context" impacts the environment in which the negotiation takes place. For example, in the demographic context one age group's bargaining power may be stronger than the other. In an aging municipality, advocacy for a senior community center may be more successful than a playground with a swing set at the park. Conversely, in a municipality full of young families, the park will win the day.

At the personal or organizational level, the negotiator's history, educational background, friends, customers, partners, socioeconomic status, culture, values and religious beliefs all provide context to impact the relationships from the first contact to the end of the negotiations. Remember, negotiation is a human endeavor.

The context analysis in negotiation occurs during our first and perhaps the most important step, which is preparation. This is the time to gather information and data to create value and tell a story or the "why" of the negotiation addressing the needs of this particular context.

Defining the context also determines the form or channel of negotiation. We identify in the paragraphs below relevant channels of direct negotiations, negotiations through an agent, a facilitator, a mediator, auctions, multi stakeholder dialogue and parallel informal negotiations.

Direct negotiations are appropriate between friends or organizations with existing relationships. The social capital already in place between two friends is all that may be necessary to at least begin direct negotiations. Newgotiations through an agent like a real estate agent, lawyer or trade union, facilitate more distant relationships or perhaps relationships in need of technical expertise like law. In other words, a functional relationship between actors bound by a social structure may be used to produce an economic or non-economic outcome.

In the context of an environmental dispute two competing organizations may request a neutral facilitator to advance negotiations. Facilitators like the United Nations, World Bank or NGO's like Doctors Without Borders, Red Cross, are useful in negotiations, public policy and administration. Their established social and human capital helps them design and implement needed administrative remedies in negotiations between countries or international organizations.

Newgotiations through a neutral Mediator is to resolve legal disputes. An entire field of Alternative Dispute Resolution is becoming a precious tool for bench officers, judges and trained lawyers to mediate disputes. In a context where there is not much to negotiate but price, like a commodity or public procurement, auctions provide the best form or channel for negotiation. The electronic auctions like EBay, E*TRADE or Bloomberg help supply and demand in an efficient and productive manner. While our Newgotiation model may be used to improve relations between suppliers and customers, in buying and selling products, auctions to conclude the transaction remain the most efficient channel and are not what we are addressing in this book.

Yet another form or channel of Newgotiation is the multi stakeholder dialogue in a more 21st century collaborative context. We argue that the three sectors are more predisposed to collaborate than ever before due to various contextual settings like the new media, Internet and globalization. Nicolas Berggruen in his book "Intelligent Governance for the 21st Century" suggests that in a genuinely multi-polar world there is no single power that dominates the bargain. He further argues that a new system of "intelligent governance" is required to meet these new challenges. The North Korean missile crisis of 2017 illustrates the difficulties of this context and the importance of multi-lateral relationships and discussions with various stakeholders. During his last visit to the United States, French president Emmanuel Macron emphatically made his case for multilateralism for most challenges facing the world today.

The Multi Stakeholder Dialogue provides the platform for the exchange of ideas to harmonize beliefs, interests and convictions to reach a collaborative state and result. This is more useful in framing. Last but not least, parallel informal negotiations may be useful in more delicate potentially hopeless public negotiations. If it were not for this direct but parallel approach through informal channels to President Kennedy by a representative of General Secretary Khrushchev, history tells us that there may not have been an aversion of the Cuban Missile Crisis. As we know, the crisis ended with Russia agreeing to remove the missiles from Cuba. In return, for the United States agreeing to remove Jupiter missiles from Turkey and Italy and pledging to not invade Cuba.

Interest

Our second element "interest" is all about defining the "why" or the purpose for our negotiation. Why are we here? In our Newgotiation paradigm the general answer is always to maximize the value of our cooperation and to create a sustainable long-term relationship. In other words, defining the win/win approach begins right here.

Interest from a technical sense is defined in our preparation and value creation steps. Interest is our mission, our vision, goals and the target that we want to achieve through this process. If interest were only about price, it would be single dimensional, a one-sided definition of purpose leading to a very short win/lose frame or at best a compromise between the contemplated price A and price B.

We want more in a multi-lateral and integral negotiations. In fact, as Public Administration Professionals in the 21st century we cannot afford less. Our constituencies are demanding more effective, efficient, cost prudent, successful and sustainable collaborations. Our Newgotiation paradigm addresses these needs. Notice for this element we said "interest" and not "position." Interest defines the problem and motivates people to find solutions to the problem. Interest is defined as, "something that concerns, involves, draws the attention of, or arouses the curiosity of a person."

Every interest has several potential solutions that could satisfy it. Behind opposed positions lie shared and compatible interests. Each side has multiple interests, but they also have basic human needs consistent with their personal characteristics we discussed earlier. A good Newgotiator acknowledges the other side's interest and attacks the problem without blaming them. Separating the people from the problem allows the parties to address the issues without damaging their relationship. It also helps them to get a clearer view of the substantive problem that may need a good solution satisfactory to both.

Emotions are a second source of people problems. Negotiation can be a frustrating process. People often react with fear or anger when they feel that their interests are threatened. Our Newgotiators are good and empathetic listeners, who give the speaker their full attention, occasionally respectfully and accurately summarizing the speaker's points to confirm their understanding.

Generally, the principled Newgotiator uses questions and strategic silences to draw the other party out to discover more. Discussions look forward to the desired solution, rather than focusing on past events. Sometime the solutions are simple but not readily apparent. Only a good listener can pick up the nuances of various interests to satisfy. In illustrating this aspect of Newgotiation, we typically provide our students with the following hypothetical case study, dilemma and proposed solution:

Daniel has been a dedicated, hardworking, honest, productive employee of the city for over 15 years. His children were born right before he joined the city. He now has asked his city manager Nicole for a 5% raise. The city has been hit hard with the recent recession with the loss of jobs, declining tax revenues, additional unfunded mandates and loss of redevelopment laws. While the economy is rebounding slowly the city council has asked the city manager to remain vigilant and frugal.

We then ask our students to address the negotiation dilemma in a role play exercise. We see varied results during this exercise. One result is to simply decline Daniel's request for good but unfortunate fiscal reason. However, this result yields an extremely disappointed and demoralized 15-year loyal employee. Another is to negotiate a more modest increase. Daniel is somewhat happy but is still hurt that his loyalty and hard work is worth substantially less than 5%. And yet another after quite a bit of discussion about various interests yields no raise but Daniel and Nicole claim to be very happy with the result. The proverbial win/win.

While the third scenario seems puzzling, we as observers are never surprised. The third group typically begins the negotiation by discussing Daniel's good service to the city, his dedication and time spent at work. The fiscal realities of the city—despite everyone's good work and the blessings of long-term employment as well as the camaraderie forged in the process. A discussion takes place about his family and the needs of his family. The group typically reports that Daniel wished that he spent more time with his children who are growing and soon ready to go to college. Through this discussion, the city manager is able to fashion a win/win solution to the dilemma. A Newgotiator and an empathetic listener, Nicole offers Daniel a flex weekly schedule allowing Daniel to take every other Friday off to be with his family. No increase or decrease in pay. Daniel is happy to be able to spend more time with his family. Nicole is happy and so is the city council for not having to pay more money. Nicole remains Daniel's favorite city manager and remains devoted to public service in the city.

In our world of Newgotiation, parties keep a clear focus on their interests, but remain open to different proposals and solutions. Interests are critical to the discussion of options, but premature judgment hinders imagination, creativity, innovation and the quest to think outside the box to come up with solutions. In our case study, Nicole's ability to put her finger on the problem through empathy (i.e. needing time to spend with children) solves the dilemma with a satisfied long-term employee.

Newgotiation accomplishes balancing interests as it is predisposed to seek the "why" or "why this project?" Frank often tells his real estate development master's students that gracing us with their presence as developers in our municipalities is simply not enough to serve all interests including those of our constituents. Yet bureaucratizing our municipalities is not in their or our interest either. This is where we need a collaborative approach as opposed to an adversarial approach. This is where through the same exercise of good listening skills, we come up with imaginative, creative and innovative solutions to deal with all of our interests including creating or maintaining parks, open space, storm drains, traffic, climate change concerns and of course the monetary profit interest of the developer. Profits in this context are not measured by just dollars and cents or by sectors, but by benefits to all project participants including the municipality. Public Administration Professionals as Newgotiators fundamentally focus on these benefits to better serve their constituencies.

Transitioning from the preparation step to value creation is an interesting brainstorming process. The discussion about interest in defining mission, vision and goals transform into a discussion about joint mission, joint vision and joint targets. The development of a definition of joint purpose, search for mutual gains and inventing ways of making decisions easy are conducive to value creation and ultimately value distribution in our system of Newgotiation. A good stakeholder analysis and overall preparation facilitates this process.

All this being said it would be naïve to think and approach any negotiation without a plan "B." Remember it is all about the frame. William Uyr, Roger Fisher and Bruce Patton call this Best Alternative to a Negotiated Agreement or BATNA. BATNA gives us the power to walk away if we are unable to reach mutual gains at any stage of the negotiation. The better the BATNA the stronger our ability to negotiate. However, in our paradigm of Newgotiation, we advocate the use of BATNA as a tool to collaborate and strengthen the deal at hand rather than a tool to support walking away.

To illustrate our point, we offer the following hypothetical scenario between two technology sector giants, Intel and Hewlett Packard (HP). Let us consider that HP offers to buy 1 million Intel processors. Intel offers the price of $100 per sourced processor for a total contract price of $100 million dollars. If HP were willing to pay $80 million dollars, we know that the ZOPA is valued at $20 million dollars.

We expect these two sophisticated Fortune 100 companies to always come to the negotiation table with a BATNA. We would imagine for this transaction, IBM (another computer maker) in the case of Intel, and perhaps ARM (another processor manufacturer) in the case of HP. These BATNA's give each organization the opportunity to walk away in the case of no agreement on ZOPA.

Under our paradigm of Newgotiation, however, we expect Intel and HP to engage each other to discuss their respective interests not just as a supplier (Intel) and purchaser (HP) but also as two technology giants with enormous potentials to develop viable and sustainable options to work with each other to improve the "size of the pie." Some of these interests include buying and selling their respective products, joint advertising, research and development collaborations, cash flow management vis a vis sales and joint branding. The sticker that we see in many PC's today with the statement "Intel inside," is in fact a product of interest-based negotiations. Branding its product was a substantial goal of Intel, for which it was willing to forge a long-term relationship with HP and sell processors for a better price. More importantly both organizations through the relationship benefit to this day in augmenting the size of their transactions or the size of the "pie." These interests create value beyond the $20 million-dollar ZOPA. These interests invent for the negotiators amazing opportunities to improve the capacity of the deal.

We envision the same outcome, for example, in entitling a 64-unit condominium complex in a local municipality. First the BATNA; there is always another developer. However, if this entitlement is only about development fees and established land use like 40 units per acre for example, reaching ZOPA is quick and there is either a deal or no deal.

In our Newgotiation paradigm this is not just about a 64-unit condominium complex. This is about the beautification, economic development, housing and advancement of the community. This is perhaps about undergrounding of utilities, fixing storm drains and creating renewables like solar energy, density bonuses for affordability and a pocket park at or near the site. In other words, "why this project?"

What Newgotiation teaches to companies like HP, Sony, Monsanto, Johnson & Johnson or Praxair/White Martins, Katerra Construction or mayors and council members in our Local Leaders Forum at University of Southern California is to learn how to postpone the moment of doing the anchoring of the price (only at value distribution step) by discussing interests, creating options to improve the probability to close a better deal.

Options

The third element in our 4-10-10 system is "options." Like context and interest, options are created in our Newgotiation steps one (preparation) and step two (value creation.) Options are about imagination, creativity and innovation. Finding elegant options for the interests we create in the previous step of our Newgotiation process is what makes Newgotiation pleasant. There is no tension or friction here, only opportunity to solve problems through creativity.

This element is about building a rapport, personalizing, customizing and matching interests with options for solutions. This element is about "enlarging the size of the pie" before dividing the pie in our next Newgotiation step of value distribution. A word of caution here is appropriate. Collaboration in our Newgotiation context does not mean capitulation. A good Newgotiator assures that there are sufficient options for both sides to distribute and more importantly never reveals the order of importance of each option. Walking away from the wrong frame is critical. This is also where BATNA comes in to help shape these options.

Finally, options and various alternatives to those options add value and improve our ability to cut a better deal. The more options the easier the distribution and the more room for concessions in ideal deal making. Uneven option creation yields disproportionate concessions. The purpose of our Newgotiation paradigm is equitable and balanced distribution of options. The win/win opportunity demands nothing less.

Power

Our fourth element, "power" is potentially more destructive than constructive or productive. However, "power," especially for our Public Administration Professionals is very much part of every negotiation and relationship in some form or another. We, therefore, spend several cautionary pages to identify the minefield. We also qualify our discussion about power in three distinct categories as in self-centered motivations, tactics that misfire because they damage relationships and qualities that lubricate negotiations because they improve relationships.

Self-centered motivations

The power of money helps us determine authority and ability to transact a deal, but it also helps to corrupt. The power of money, like the power of sex, is an incredible source of influence. Moreover, either power is quite addictive. The chemical imbalance they provide for the human brain removes the capacity to fear or adhere to civil society rules, norms or laws.

Unfortunately, the power of money and sex are the two most dangerous causes of disgrace for Public Administration Professionals. We have known presidents, governors, ministers, legislators, mayors and council members lose the trust of their constituents and sometimes their office because of the addictive and destructive nature of these kinds of power. This is one more reason why our Newgotiation technique focuses on the purpose of the negotiation rather than the price. The identification of the "why" through the creation of interests and inventions of options reduce the risk of corruption or self-interest.

Purpose, particularly public purpose, grounds us and reminds us of our responsibility as public servants. Negotiating on behalf of the public for the purpose of creating value for the community in which we have the honor of serving is a collective interest. The power of money or sex is self-interest. Our Newgotiation technique is designed to pursue collaboration and cooperation to improve the deal for everyone as opposed to someone. Good governance measures such as transparency and accountability, help expose self-interest, which is a secret.

The power of ego is not a distant third to the first two that we identify here. An Egomaniac is sure of his truth being the only truth. He has difficulty to learn. More importantly he thinks that listening is a waste of time. Given that we identify listening, in fact empathetic listening as an important tool to invent solutions in our system of Newgotiation, an egomaniac is a liability in value creation. Manipulating or seducing the egomaniac with skill may be the only way to transform the negative into a positive. This is very similar to our discussion of the Authoritarian and the story of the French ambassador Talleyrand transforming the emperor of Prussia to preserve the magnificent bridge of Pont d'Alexandre III in Paris. Changing the frame is critical.

Envy and jealousy are engines of power and weakness in negotiation. Both create conflict. More importantly both lead to lose/lose outcomes. How many times have we encountered siblings fighting over a family heirloom, which gets sold in an estate sale because neither agrees for the other to have it? Being envious of the other party's benefits from the options created in the negotiation is indeed dangerous. This is the competitive frame as opposed to the more productive collaborative frame.

We discussed earlier the importance of having equal amounts of options at the value distribution stage to make sure that the negotiation leads to a win/win. We now emphasize the importance of the quality of the options created as well as the quantity. While jealousy may be used as a motivator, which may be a good thing, quality and balanced options avoid the negative and destructive human emotions of jealousy or envy.

In the context of negotiations with a real estate developer for entitlements, Frank always says that as mayor or council member, he is never negatively concerned with the potential benefits of the developer but only with the benefits of his constituents as a result of the proposed development. He looks for quality and balance in duties and responsibilities of each side. He looks for fairness and justice for his community but never envious of the benefits of the developer. He adds, the goal is to make both the developer and the community winners in the negotiated outcome. They both deserve success and our job as Public Administration Professionals is to facilitate that success.

The power of "reciprocity" is a double-edged sword. In civil society and based on our common value system we reciprocate a gift with a gift, a favor with another favor, an act of kindness with another act of compassion. "Thank you" in Brazil is expressed with the word "obrigado" which means "obliged." But being obliged to one is inconsistent with representing many.

Conflicts of interest laws are grounded on the notion that Public Administration Professionals owe paramount loyalty to the public. Thus, personal and private financial considerations on the part of Public Administration Professionals are not allowed to enter the decision-making process. While the power of reciprocity may be symbolic and even permissible if the benefit inures to all, Public Administration Professionals must value integrity and ethics in our Newgotiations and stay away from even the perception of potential reciprocity if reciprocity includes self-interest over the interest of the public.

Tactics that misfire because they damage relationships

The power of the threat can be productive if used properly. Confidence, posture and the skill to dissuade are great resources to avoid a conflict or a fight. The old Roman adage "si vis pacem para bellum" or "if you want peace prepare for war," in its right context demonstrates the power of the general threat to be prepared for the accomplishment of the good. On the other hand, specific threats frustrate the collaborative approach and reduce the chances of prolonged discussions for the creation of interests and inventions of options to solve problems.

The power of the bluff like the tactic of domination in negotiation can work but it is short lived. Bluffing may be a skill for a poker game but complex negotiations for our organizations or our communities are no game. Pretending through silence or misrepresentation, ruins social capital and reputation not to mention that it is simply dishonest. It takes years to build trust and reputation and one bluff to destroy them. And for those who think they got away, there is always next time and once discovered, suspicion plagues that relationship forever. We unequivocally believe that this is not for our Public Administration Professionals. We always advocate ethics before anything else in our Newgotiation. No deal is worth compromising our reputation or integrity. Perhaps another way of saying this is that bluff and misrepresentation cannot possible achieve the opportunity to win/win, especially in the long term.

Among the powers that are not helpful to our paradigm of Newgotiation is what old negotiators call "salami tactics." This is a tool to manipulate more than collaborate. It consists of making the negotiation last as a step-by-step process, forcing small concessions in "thinly cut slices." In our classes, we create a set of learning tools by gathering intelligence and information in our preparation step to avoid being the victim of such archaic power tactics. Also, the use of a facilitator with social capital is helpful to change the narrative from manipulation to collaboration. These tactics do not add value but detract to only destroy trust.

Another dreadful power trick in the old repertoire of negotiation is the unwelcomed and unsolicited "last bid." Asking yet another concession before signing off on long and sometimes painful negotiations is a power tactic. It is dishonest and undermines collaboration and ruins any trust that may have been built during the negotiation process. This tactic is short sided and will surely ruin reputation. One way to respond is to revisit the interests in an attempt to reset the negotiation. This may also be a great place to use BATNA to either recast the agreed deal or potentially walk away.

Perhaps the most classic power tactic of old negotiators is what is called "good cop and bad cop." Put in practice by the cooperative and competitive side of negotiation in one. This 2 in 1 strategy does not help relationship or reputation building either. It is inconsistent with our ethical and elegant standards to strive for the collaborative win/win. In fact, the "bad cop" is intentionally looking to intimidate through deception.

We see this as the opposite of our Newgotiation paradigm where both parties win through sharing. To defuse such an ugly scenario, honesty in labeling and diplomatically exposing the tactic with a request to start over is beneficial. Assurances that all interests are discussed openly and fairly are persuasive. Good preparation and the power of anticipation are good tools to avoid the tactic all together. Our purposeful, methodic and thoughtful preparation leads us to negotiate with one person with authority or legitimacy, building trust and avoiding the bad cop all together. If this tactic persists, bringing your own bad cop may be a reminder that a reset of the relationship may be helpful to all.

Qualities that lubricate negotiations because they improve relationships

The power of media and more importantly new media is quite remarkable and undeniably potent. Image, or more importantly reputation and the intangible value it provides to various actors in Newgotiations is substantially enhanced or otherwise affected by media. We must pay attention to this power and use it to promote the value of the win/win.

In an increasingly competitive environment - as companies fight for revenue, growth, market share and loyalty - measuring and managing corporate reputation has become the key driver of business value. Although most companies agree that reputation management is important, relatively few have figured out how to harness its value. While almost 80% of companies polled agree that we now live in a "Reputation Economy," a marketplace where who you are matters more than what you produce, however, only 20% say their company is ready to compete in it.

The battle for corporate social responsibility is being waged across the globe. Google tops this chart according to the Reputation Institute Report of 2014, with over $353 million in grants worldwide, $3 billion in free ads, apps and products, and Google employees volunteering approximately 6,200 total days of employee time to support nonprofits (a total of 150,000 hours). We find this intangible value of the image helpful to our new paradigm of increasingly distributed or shared governance, which in turn promotes the opportunity to a win/win. Reputation creates trust and trust creates deals.

Next in our review is the valuable power of social capital. The World Bank defines social capital as "institutions, relationships, and norms that shape the quality and quantity of a society's social interactions." In an article that we assign in our classes about "Social Capital in the Creation of Human Capital" James S. Coleman writes, "Social capital is productive, making possible the achievement of certain ends that in its absence would not be possible." We believe this productivity is paramount in our Newgotiation. Social scientists conclude that social capital improves economic, political, administrative and overall human behaviors because indeed it is comprised of concepts such as "trust", "community" and "networks."

While these concepts are difficult to quantify, the challenge is increased when one seeks to measure not just the quantity but also the quality of social capital on a variety of scales. The World Bank encourages social scientists to identify methods and tools to qualify and quantify social capital so that policy makers are able to make decisions about subjects like poverty, economic development and democracy.

Results in the qualification and quantification of social capital are fascinating. Measures of trust in government or interpersonal trust, strong voting trends, membership in civic organizations and volunteerism all contribute to the prosperity of a city, state or nation. John F. Helliwell and Robert D. Putnam in the Eastern Economic Journal (1995) examine social capital comparing north and south Italy. Their research and conclusions support social scientists and are quite compelling about the power of social capital. In Northern Italy, where indicators like civic involvement, voter turnout, newspaper readership, membership in organizations such as football clubs and confidence in public institutions are high, significant improvement in governance is shown compared to struggling Southern Italy, which is much poorer and more disengaged from government and institutions.

In simple terms, there is no substitute for trust, community or networks when seeking to improve the probability of closing a better deal, improve value through collaboration, improve productivity by sharing and prevent conflict. There is no better way to Newgotiate than "putting an arm" around someone we know in our community or network that we trust to describe the "why."

Starting with similar interests is more than half the battle in negotiations. In this context, World Bank's research finds "increasing evidence that social cohesion is critical for societies to prosper economically and for development to be sustainable. Social capital is not just the sum of the institutions, which underpin a society – it is the glue that holds them together."

Moreover, our leadership in trust assures happier Newgotiations and happier communities. Stéphane Garelli is a Professor at both International Institute for Management Development (IMD) and the University of Lausanne. He leads the team, which publishes the IMD World Competitiveness Yearbook - the most comprehensive and reputed study in the field of the competitiveness of nations. Not surprisingly countries with high interpersonal trust rank among the top 10 prosperous in the world. Happiness is very high among the Nordic countries. Sweden ranks at about the same level as Norway and Finland, but after Denmark. The United States among the countries with more than 150 million people ranks number 10.

Our Newgotiation paradigm thrives on trust, social capital, integrity, elegance and ethics. Our Newgotiators have a higher success rate to strike a better deal. This being said we do not advocate naiveté either. When facing negative power tactics good Newgotiators anticipate what may be missing. Max H. Bazerman and Michael D. Watkins in their book entitled "Predictable Surprises: The Disasters You Should Have Seen Coming, and How to Prevent Them" show us in the business context how to minimize risk by understanding and lowering the psychological, organizational and political barriers preventing us from foreseeing some of the manipulations we discuss here. They then describe the powerful tools - including incentives and formal coalitions - that business or Public Administration Professionals can use to ferret out and fend off threats invisible to insiders.

Perhaps more simply put is the Old Russian proverb adopted by an American President Ronald Reagan, "trust but verify." This phrase has since passed into the American lexicon to simply warn against predictable surprises. Negotiators need to foster this reasonable sense of suspicion by asking through trusted channels, relations and networks the veracity of the information provided during preparation. In our technique, accurate information is key to identifying interests, making decisions, developing options and designing elegant solutions to distribute during our value distribution step.

The Harvard Business Review reports on this new principal of shared value, which involves "creating economic value in a way that also creates value for society by addressing its needs and challenges." This is perhaps the power of empathy and care, not quite seen or practiced before. Companies are reconnecting their success with social progress.

Shared value is not necessarily social responsibility or philanthropy, but a new standard to achieve economic success. A growing number of companies known for their business savvy and accomplishments such as GE, Google, IBM, Intel, Johnson & Johnson, Nestlé, Unilever, Costco and Wal-Mart have already embarked on significant efforts to create shared value by restructuring the intersection between society and corporate performance and success.

In our classes for intersectoral leadership we are teaching and imploring the government leaders of tomorrow to wisely regulate in ways that enable shared value rather than deter it. This overall theme of empathy or empathetic listening to address needs and challenges through our Newgotiation technique should not come as a surprise to our readers by now. Newgotiation is all about empathetic listening to align interests, create options and invent solutions. One of our favorite quotes from the Greek philosopher Epictetus is "We have two ears and one mouth so that we can listen twice as much as we speak." This remains by far one of the best pieces of advice we give our students.

Our colleague Robert Denhardt in his book Just Plain Good Management, starts lesson one with "[L]isten, listen, listen. The first and most important idea in good management is simple: listen, listen, listen. Failure to listen attentively, genuinely, thoughtfully and completely is the cause of an incredible number of organizational breakdowns. On the other hand, listening carefully builds trust, engagement and, in turn, productivity. Practice not just hearing but really listening to others. Encourage people to listen to each other. And, who knows, people might even listen to you." We agree. Perhaps more impactful than lesson one, Professor Denhardt concludes, "remember the first lesson of management: listen, listen, listen. Assuming you've got that down, now give it a twist. Listen empathetically." He continues, "Walk a mile in their shoes, even if their shoes don't quite fit and are the wrong color. Sympathize, empathize – but then take the next step." These are lessons that clearly fit what we teach in Newgotiation, because failure to empathetically listen in the preparation and value creation steps of the technique we describe in this book, leads to missed opportunities to create value. Lack of value decreases the probability to close a better deal.

Aside listening, we think of intuition as a magical phenomenon—but what many call "gut instincts" are formed out of our past experiences and knowledge developed over time. One can develop her intuitive capabilities by being perceptive, attentive, detail oriented, curious and repetitive.

Many studies show that average learning retention rates from a lecture is about 5%; by contrast the retention rate by actually doing substantially increases the rate to 75%. Those that are trained in the FBI, general law enforcement or Custom and Border Control academies master these skills by doing, where they develop an intuition about a person who is lying or is embarrassed or hiding something.

In more recent psychology, intuition can embody the skill to come up with fast and effective solutions to problems, the importance of which in our paradigm we discussed in the creation of options. Gary Kline, a pioneer in the field of natural decision-making found that under time pressures and fluid conditions, experts use their "base of experience to identify similar situations and intuitively [choose] feasible solutions." Developing these skills are at the core of our Newgotiation paradigm. Finding feasible and elegant solutions is what we teach for value creation and ultimately value distribution. In our experience, we find that intuitive negotiators are better at finding and negotiating a better deal. Steve Jobs said, "have the courage to follow your heart and intuition. They somehow know what you truly want to become."

Last but not least the power of humor is of course a great strategy to captivate and to be enchanting. We teach our students and trainees to be entertaining and not boring during their presentations. We insist on crisp and yet informative presentations delivered with charm to draw others into our stories. Some call this charisma. We describe it as the ability to enlighten the part of the brain that makes people feel positive and enthused. When participants to a negotiation smile and dream, studies show that the results are very positive.

In our classes, we practice story telling peppered with clean and understandable humor. We encourage our students to be passionate about their stories. Passion shows that we care. And when we care we listen. When we listen, we learn about interests and potential problems attached to those interests. When we know the problems, only then can we invent solutions. The more elegant and collaborative the solutions we invent, the higher the chances of a deal. The more elegant and collaborative solution we develop the higher the chances of a better deal. Our paradigm of Newgotiation is all about the value added and the "better deal."

Communication

Story telling nicely correlates to our 5th element to pilot Newgotiations through effective communication. Spoken, unspoken and written communication remains a very important element of our Newgotiation paradigm. Given that we focus on the "why" by telling a story, writing skills, presentation and presentation skills are paramount for a successful negotiator. First impressions count for a lot and sometimes first bad impression is irreversible. The elements of communication and relationship, which we will discuss next, are the two out of our 10 elements that have applications in all of our four steps for Newgotiation (i.e. Preparation, Value Creation, Value Distribution and Implementation or Follow Through).

There is nothing more important than preparation to know how to communicate effectively and efficiently. Our investigation or preparation before beginning the negotiation must ascertain the identity and characteristics of our negotiating partner(s), context including the impact of culture, values, acquaintances, networks and habits. For instance, based on our own experience in teaching or coaching in various countries or to various cultures, we find clear differences and tendencies in communication. In Nigeria, top down negotiations are the norm. In China, a trusted facilitator is preferred. In France, social status, job title and educational credentials make a substantial difference in the negotiation process. Also, political context or image cannot be ignored in communication. Negotiation with a "labor party Mayor" for a Labor Day celebration in Brazil will most likely not succeed if the negotiator shows up in a designer suit, attaché and expensive watch. 80% of communication is non-verbal so we must consider our appearance, mannerisms and gestures during negotiations.

Displaying elegance, passion, care and consideration goes a long way. The perception and reality of civility make good impression and help start the branding and collaborative process for our negotiation. Making others feel important is a special skill that rewards the participant in our Newgotiation paradigm. The number one reason for an employee to leave his job is not the money or the work but his relationship with his superiors and colleagues. Nurturing that relationship from day one is extremely important in the negotiation process.

The use of technology to communicate is now quite acceptable in all circles. Visual and Audio presentations to present documents, slides, or any other type of media must look and feel professional. This is typically our first impression after our physical appearance. We insist with our students to consider design criteria with slides. Where to locate logos on a consistent basis? How to deal with images to tell a story? How not to overload presentations with text or numbers? How to use pleasant color pallets? How to choose a location for the presentation? Above all how to clearly and linearly communicate the "why," the "what," and the "how" of the given project or the substance of the negotiation, in that order.

The first minute in a digital presentation as well as a conversation is critical to the outcome. Ricardo Bellino in his book "You have Three Minutes!" offers his successful wisdom on the impact of the first impression, the power of intuition and the importance of image and nonverbal behaviors. These are all things that we embrace in our Newgotiation paradigm.

Consistency and commitment communicate trust and trust builds reputation. To succeed in negotiations, we need both. We previously discussed trust in the context of building social capital and the importance of social capital in improving our ability to transact a deal. In our world of Newgotiation, there is nothing like the success of a closed deal, influencing the next deal. Public Administration Professionals often say correctly implementation is everything!

Soft diplomacy and moral elegance are part of the research Yann conducted during his postdoctoral work at Harvard. Researchers and practitioners are always intrigued to know how to deal with critical communicative moments during a negotiation. This research and the literature of communication during negotiations provide a guide to best practices. A non-comprehensive but instructive list for our Newgotiations is as follows:

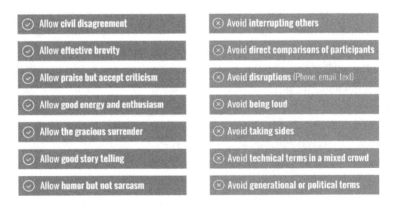

Figure 6.2

Proper communication is paramount in telling the story, describing interests, finding and applying solutions and even in determining the hypothesis of the problem or the subject matter of the negotiation. What could be critically and fatally flawed is a miscommunication on the hypothesis. In other words, how can we solve a problem if we do not agree on the definition?

The "what" is important for two reasons. One is to operate from the same definition to define interests. The other is to customize options. Buying oranges for a juice manufacturer is different than buying oranges for a bakery. One needs the pulp, the other the skin. A collaborative approach to buying the same orange may yield substantial benefits and therefore a better deal for the farmer, juicer and baker.

Here the value creation step is to connect interests, preferences and options to harness a better deal. The etymology and the epistemology are key to effective communication. For this reason, we see Newgotiation using framing knowledge management, as a way of reducing the gap between information and perception, which is a source of disagreement.

Our culture of Newgotiation focuses more on the cognitive tools we describe in this book and on resolving any differences in an elegant manner. The empathetic listener and the elegant Newgotiator would say "here is how I see this, if I am wrong please help me see it differently." This statement is authentic, honest and truthful. This is about joint fact finding and not about persuasion or advocacy. The exercise is all about reducing the gap between perception and reality so that both parties have accurate data to craft options and solve problems. No one benefits from a deal constructed on a false premise or bad decisions. This is where the elements of good decision making as articulated by our colleague Professor Abbas become so important.

Relationship

Our sixth element in our Newgotiation technique is relationship. This includes people at the negotiation table as well as people who can affect the outcome of the negotiation. This is quite multidimensional for our Public Administration Professionals. Having existing and forging relationships with various stakeholders are common practices for Public Administration Professionals. Building trust and acceptance among stakeholders is not only important but also necessary for public negotiations. To amass a comprehensive list of stakeholders for the purpose of developing the necessary relations and data for negotiations we offer the following strategies:

1. Involve internal stakeholders, also known as city or relevant government staff as early and as frequently as possible. They are professionals with amazing resources. The more involved they feel, the more they are invested in the idea and the more likely they are to agree with the direction of the prospective negotiation. Additionally, the earlier they are involved, the earlier you can address their needs and concerns as opposed to discovering them late into the process. These are people who are responsible for carrying out policy decisions made by you.

2. Set proper metrics and expectations before work begins for the preparation of the negotiation. Clear directions, metrics and reasonable expectations engender trust improving the chances of success.

3. Identify key staff to build a team but don't ignore the rest. It is critical to recognize everyone's agendas, goals and expectations, while making sure to include staff at all levels. Addressing staff's needs helps gain momentum from the bottom up and ensures that we tackle potential concerns from all directions during our preparation.

4. Tell stories and walk through scenarios when presenting policy or projects. Stories bring meaning and value beyond how policy or projects appear on the surface. Stories help us establish a connection with our staff on both analytical and emotional levels and can be very effective not only in our preparation but also in value creation and value distribution steps of Newgotiation.

5. Express tradeoffs that occur if policy or projects compromises are made. Whenever someone questions the approach or suggests an alternative way of doing things, be ready to explain elegantly the tradeoffs that will occur if those changes are made. For example, while something may be cheaper and easier to build, an increase in usability issues may ultimately affect the overall conversation. Feedback is not always a negative compromise. Many times, stakeholder feedback can result in beneficial gains to the user experience and product success. Embrace options.

6. Relate ideas and policy or projects back to the needs of stakeholders. When presenting policy or projects, keep in mind the perspective of the stakeholders or constituents at large. These are people who will be impacted by the decision of the policy makers. These are also people who have an emotional or relational interest in the policy outcomes.

7. Support policy or projects with data whenever possible to reduce subjectivity. Policy or projects should be influenced (not necessarily "driven") by data. While not everything can be influenced by data, being able to refer to both qualitative and quantitative research that helped influence the approach can be very helpful in reducing subjective opinions during policy or project discussions.

8. Speak their language. This will help you connect with your stakeholder audience and will help stakeholders focus on what's really important. Ultimately this is important to build competency, relationship and trust.

9. Don't be overly defensive or let pride get in the way. Stakeholders offer a very important perspective and their insights are critical to the success of the project. If feedback comes off as critical without being constructive, generally it's because it's difficult to articulate what doesn't feel right about a policy or projects. Listen actively to all feedback and try to focus on what the real issues are as opposed to always jumping to defend an established position. Those of us in public office know very well the embarrassment we feel when a position we advocate is destroyed by facts and figures during a public hearing process by ordinary citizens. Back to Professor Denhardt's lesson "listen, listen, listen."

10. Communicate well. It may be best to present diagrams and storyboards to help visualize ideas and to tell the larger story.

11. Offer methods of testing various approaches when consensus cannot be reached. There are times when stakeholder feedback may seem perfectly valid, but there's no clear way of determining whether one idea or approach is better than another. An informal mediation may be a viable solution. The more options, the more chances to settle or mediate desired outcomes.

12. Foresee and address technical concerns. Consult with technical experts as often as needed, as technical mistakes are easy to make but difficult to correct

once the negotiation is in progress. These are people who have knowledge or information needed for you to make good policy decisions. Help them help you.

13. Engage people whose different ways of thinking or working bring novel ideas to the process and to the policymaking. Think different said Steve Jobs, "if you don't cannibalize yourself, someone else will." Most importantly remember important resources like the youth.

Conformity to the Rule of Law

The ultimate facilitator or constrain for negotiations is the rule of law. The use of the law in negotiations is much more strategic in nature. Deep knowledge and understanding of laws may facilitate negotiations by allowing Public Administration Professionals to shape legal interests, for better options and solutions within the bounds of the law. By the same token the rule of law is a limitation for the contemplated negotiation process as well as the expected outcome.

For example, even assuming the necessity of pension reform for the financial health of a municipal organization, the law may prohibit those reforms or the collective bargaining agreement in place may bar reduction of previously bargained and vested benefits. Legal compliance, including authority to contract has a direct impact on the credibility and leadership of the public leader. Better to know at the outset if the subject matter of the negotiation is legally achievable. Therefore, consulting a lawyer is necessary for a public leader during the preparation phase and ultimately implementation or follow through phase of the negotiation.

We offer a caveat here about what we generally mean by the use of the word "legally." Clearly, we mean the literal compliance with law, but we also mean compliance with local customs, conventions and behavioral expectations. Especially in the public domain, the role of politics is substantial and perceptions in politics is reality. Adhering to these customs and expectations must be part of the preparation step as well as implementation.

In our ethics or leadership classes we typically teach that the law is the minimum requirement. So just because it is legal it does not mean that it is ethical or customary. Granting a contract to a friend's company in which the public leader has no financial interest may be legal but not necessarily acceptable for the constituents of the public leader in the United States. And of course, geographic context, like your own home and neighborhood, also adds yet another dimension to what normal or legally acceptable behavior or interaction may be.

For example, what may constitute sexual harassment in the United States may be culturally and legally acceptable in Europe. Therefore, the broader legal requirements contemplated and mapped by trained facilitators like lawyers have a great impact on preparation and ultimately the outcome of each negotiation.

The impact during preparation may also be about assessment of the laws in terms of risks, investments and need for interventions for different laws. If the negotiation is about to invest in a country like Brazil for instance, labor laws, social security, tax laws have a great impact on the preparation about the decision to invest. The law and customs about self-interest, conflicts, courts and the time it takes to resolve disputes may also be of great importance during preparation.

The lack of laws or the need for different laws will always influence negotiation strategy. Industries with strong lobbies shape laws to their advantage to negotiate better deals. Sizable corporations as well as trade unions are known to use this tool quite effectively. We withhold judgment as to whether or not this tool enhances our Newgotiation paradigm. Suffice it to say that if the aim of the proposed law is for the win/win then we are comfortable in its use.

Last but not least, legal compliance assures integrity. Respect for the law demonstrates discipline. Integrity and discipline build reputation and brand. Reputation builds trust and facilitates sustainability. We teach and preach the win/win paradigm in every negotiation for our Public Administration Professionals.

Our eighth element for the Newgotiation technique is what we generally call "standards." For the most part Public Administration Professionals are generalists about overall knowledge that deals with public policy and public administration. While most American legislators are lawyers by profession, that is not necessarily true at various municipal levels. Some mayors and council members are lawyers but first and foremost they are respected members of their communities, which presumably elect them for their name identification and status in the community as a reliable individual with a good reputation. Public Administration Professionals at the local level could be lawyers, doctors, plumbers, electricians, teachers and first responders to name a few. However, for the most part, they all rely on experts to influence their decisions about policy and administration.

Consulted experts can influence negotiations when and if they are asked. Therefore, some standards are necessary to appreciate the value of the expertise provided. Standards are reviewed in our preparation step, then in the value distribution step, especially to anchor the price and finally during implementation. Solid and reliable standards help our negotiation process by improving interests, alternatives, options and legal compliance. We write few pages here to describe various known examples of standards that influence public policy and administration and therefore, the negotiation.

Standards

The market standard is typically the voice of the market or people through polls, statistics and averages. For example, it would be irresponsible to negotiate the hiring of a new city manager without knowing the market standard for a city manager with say 10 years of experience. This standard can relate to competence as well as monetary value.

Market research organizations or publication like "Consumer Guides" have developed an entire science about this standard to influence buyers of products. In the financial sector, indices for almost every conceivable part of the stock market influence all types of investors to participate in the overall economy. Investors in general are familiar with these indices through index funds and exchange traded funds which track the performance of a particular index. Dow Jones Industrial Average, New York Stock Exchange, Standard and Poor Financial, Wilshire 5000, Russell 2000, Nasdaq 100 are all examples of widely acceptable and reputable indices. These guides and indices are used as standard bearers in negotiations dealing with the markets they represent.

As in the example of the "Consumer Guides" objectivity is of utmost importance to be credible and sustainable in the expertise provided. Objective market standards provide strong tools for our Newgotiation process and our Newgotiators. These standards frame the "what" and the "how" in our process. They are proof of the truth, fairness and neutrality in our discussions to close a deal. They are also extremely helpful to some of our Newgotiators based on their identified characteristics or typology that we discussed in an earlier chapter. The controller for example will clearly find comfort in these standards. On the other hand, the visionary will most likely gloss over them requiring more on the creative or the "why" side of the column to be persuaded in the negotiation.

Accounting and management standards are also pivotal in some negotiations. Accounting is not a perfect science, in that various outcomes can be obtained depending on who and what is doing the accounting. Governments have typically observed as a standard what we call generally accepted accounting principles. In the United States the phrase "generally accepted accounting principles" (or "GAAP") consists of the basic accounting principles and guidelines with detailed rules and standards issued by the federal agency in charge of regulating the industry. The GAAP is exceedingly useful because it attempts to standardize and regulate accounting definitions, assumptions and methods bringing consistency from year to year in the methods used to prepare a public company's financial statements. The GAAP is also useful in this context to establish a standard of trust.

Management standards in the 21st century is all about the collection and distribution of data through behavioral principals that benefit and define an organization. Technology is a significant tool to manage, control, influence and facilitate negotiations. An organization like Google is constantly searching for data to customize its products and services and presumably deliver a better deal.

In our Newgotiation paradigm, where collaboration and collaborative governance is key, the management standard provides amazing analytical and practical opportunities to our Newgotiators. We highly recommend the use of this standard to add value to any deal that benefits from good data. Public Administration Professionals have an incredible resource in their own governments, which goes untapped in the preparation for most negotiations. Tap your data and analytics to prepare better and to better create value for the deal.

Simply put governments are in the data business. They know how much electricity and water we use in each dwelling unit for example. They have a record of our land ownership and land use approvals. They know what types of licenses we hold. When used properly this data yields amazing opportunities to collaborate and deliver a better deal.

In an article that Frank published with a doctoral student, entitled "From Contract Cities to Mass Collaborative Governance" they highlight several data base collaborative innovations that are becoming standards in managing municipalities and governments. Some examples from their article include, Code for America (CfA), a non-profit, which helped the city of New Orleans identify blighted properties after hurricane Katrina. Using the city's data with a sophisticated GIS technology tool CfA created a restoration-tracking tool for 35,000 abandoned properties.

Accela, a for profit organization, created Civic Insights to design a new way to visualize Palo Alto's land use permit process to make it easier and more transparent for applicants. Tumml, a nonprofit, is a startup accelerator that helps early stage companies "develop new products and services that improve urban living by connecting entrepreneurs with funding, mentors, civic leaders and a community of people dedicated to civic good." Some of their good work includes partnering with skilled workers in the trades to form a group called WorkHands, which has grown to over 5,000 registered users, who use the service to find work as well as build a reputation online. This management standard through data and technology is vastly used to defend price, objectivity, collaboration, fairness and neutrality in our Newgotiation process.

Last but not least, harmonizing standards like the accounting and management standards is part of the negotiations for example in multinational discussions. Some international mergers and acquisitions face these types of challenges. As articulated by Fisher and Ury in "Getting to Yes," the key to resolving these conflicts is to focus on objectivity and adaptation of a standard that is fair, equitable, purposeful and lawful. These are challenges that are typically overcome by highly qualified experts based on their technical knowledge and practice including organizations like CfA, Tumml and others. We encourage our Public Administration Professionals to look for these collaborations both to govern and negotiate.

Just like compliance with law, standards may also become limiting factors framing the substance of the negotiation. Manufacturing and logistics businesses are highly regulated. Therefore, not knowing the emission standards, promulgated in regulation by an air quality management district for a chemical factory or refinery, may substantially alter negotiations about locating a plant in a particular municipality. In short, collecting data, distributing data, creating patterns, procedures and standards help designing a Newgotiation strategy and also convey trust. They also help in designing elegant and informed options to negotiate better deals.

Concessions

The most common approach in conventional negotiations is positional bargaining. This is also known as the good old "haggling" in an open bazar for a product. The shop owner stakes out a high price expecting the customer to offer a very low price. After a series of concessions ZOPA is reduced to an agreed upon price or the customer moves on to the next shop owner, who represents the BATNA.

The two good arguments that can be made for this style of negotiation is that it goes back to the beginning of time and that it is rather simple. Very little preparation is necessary. It is quick and inconsequential, and it is also universally recognized and frequently used. There are also tactical and strategic benefits for one side or the other depending, which anchors the better or more favorable position.

In other words, positional bargaining has the makings of or is predisposed to be win/lose. It is competitive like arm wrestling and focuses on conflict rather than collaboration. As we previously stated this is shortsighted and certainly not sustainable in multi-lateral negotiations especially in the public sector. Perhaps most significant of its shortcomings is the lack of opportunity to discuss interests and explore more and better options or consider the "why" for the creation of the "bigger pie."

Moreover, all the benefits of collaboration, creativity and commitment to data and standards or value maximizing opportunities are completely diluted. Positional bargaining also promotes all the bad habits we discussed earlier in our power element, including salami tactics, good cop and bad cop at best, bluff and misrepresentation at worst. Positional bargaining tends to produce arbitrary results by "splitting the difference" or what might be labeled lose/lose. This outcome is very difficult for a public leader to explain to his constituency as to why he bargained to lose.

Our Newgotiation paradigm contemplates mutual concessions based on plurality of options created as a result of examined interests. Our concessions only occur at the value distribution step, which consists of transforming the package of options created without commitment during the value creation step, into a series of mutual concessions that both parties are prepared to adopt.

The value distribution step is the critical moment where Newgotiators reveal all possible options and then do the anchoring of their expected price. Value distribution is also the moment to justify price and the best available options through the use of standards, conformity to law and data. By this step our Newgotiators are expected to have established a working relationship, a level of trust, reputation, objectivity, fairness and credibility. Only then can a fair distribution of an effectively long list of balanced options be accomplished. Newgotiators use concessions to establish a distributive win/win frame.

Time

"Patience and time do more than strength or passion."

Jean de La Fontaine

"If you don't have time to do it right, when will you have time to do it over?"

John Wooden

"There are no secrets that time does not reveal."

Jean Racine

Our last but certainly not least element of our Newgotiation paradigm is time. Time is known to be one of the main sources of conflict, according to many studies. Also, time is perhaps the most undervalued commodity in the negotiation process. While positional bargaining is slow and inefficient, time is misused to make the smallest concessions to frustrate, dominate and force the marginal win/lose or even lose/lose frame.

Scholars began to realize that a more collaborative approach using time wisely and sparingly is the better approach to negotiation. One of the first publications articulating this approach is "Getting to YES" that we cited previously. Roger Fisher, William Ury and Bruce Patton articulate clearly in their book not to bargain over positions, but to separate people from problems, in order to focus on interests to invent solutions to problems using objective criteria for mutual gain. Many scholars to this day continue to follow expanding on this method including several scholars who worked with Yann to develop Newgotiations.

In Newgotiations, time is important to describe the vision or the "why". Time is important to discuss interests to create elegant options without commitment. Creativity during this process needs time. In fact, our collaborative approach explicitly delays all formal commitments or concessions towards the end of our Newgotiation process.

Time is needed to develop the relationship or build social capital between participants to explore mutually beneficial options to create and distribute value. Robert Mnookin and others point out that while the creation and distribution of value may create a tension (how much value to keep and how much to distribute) also known as the "negotiator's dilemma," studies show that through a collaborative process Newgotiators work through "gradual and reciprocal disclosure of interests while brainstorming options without commitment."

Our Newgotiation process deserves and requires time in each step. We emphasize the importance of preparation throughout our writing. Timely preparation yields a productive value creation step through the discussion of interests and the brainstorming of options without commitment. If we spend sufficient time in this last step, Public Administration Professionals will enjoy a well-balanced list of options ready for commitment through the value distribution process.

No deal is successful without implementation, which is our last step. Time in this step is a double-edged sword. On one edge is the necessity to timely implement to close and consummate the deal. On the other edge is the necessity to properly implement the agreement forged by the negotiators. Therefore, the only wisdom we can offer here is that dates and times must be set to follow through and create opportunities to meet and discuss implementation as much as possible. Regular human contact builds relations and trust.

Scheduled meetings with deliverables promote accountability and collaboration. On the other hand, we feel that it is ill advised to set deadlines to rush any Newgotiation process at the expense of our four timely and necessary steps. While there is a risk of lower productivity, we know that the probability to make a deal is higher when there is no deadline. We also know that the value of the deal tends to be larger when there is no deadline as the collaborative process facilities a better deal.

Finally, time must be evaluated in the context of culture. Some cultures appreciate and expect more time in building a relationship before transacting business and others feel that they have no time to waste with any relationship other than the business relationship to transact a deal. To be clear, we advocate a balanced and considerate approach to the element of time.

Here are few suggestions about the treatment of time as an important element in the Newgotiation process:

Be patient.

Be quick only if there is a win/win benefit in speed.

Be open to moving deadlines without abusing the practice.

Be mindful.

Be timely.

Implementation

"A good idea is about ten percent and implementation and hard work, and luck is 90 percent."

Guy Kawasaki

Our fourth step in the Newgotiation process is implementation. Implementation is defined, quite simply as "the process of putting a decision or plan into effect; execution" or as Professor Salacus calls it, "putting into action what negotiators agreed to at the bargaining table." History is full of hard negotiations that failed at this step. The most cited perhaps is the 1993 Oslo accords that negotiated peace between Israel and Palestine, only to fail in implementation. According to these definitions, implementation processes are "purposeful." They must be described in sufficient detail such that independent observers can execute without difficulty. In our Newgotiation process, implementation refers to the carrying out of the distributed options agreed to in our third step of value distribution. In fact, we are confident to say that our entire Newgotiation paradigm has no practical value without this last step.

The most negotiated and balanced elegant options for value without the implementation step or plan are just that: elegant options or plans. We need our Newgotiators to be deal makers and closers at the same time. While deal makers like Donald Trump, Michael Ovitz and Mike Cuban are revered in the eyes of the general public, their behavior as deal makers are incompatible with Public Administration Professionals. Deal makers view their responsibility to be the contract or the deal. They are less focused on the long-term execution of the deal as they rely on a group of people who pick up the pieces and attempt to make the deal work. This is not to demean these prominent deal makers but only to explain their mentality and therefore their behavior. Public Administration Professionals cannot afford to be just deal makers. They must be responsible closers as well. They are elected or appointed to be accountable for both. They must have the end in mind, raise issues early, define a joint communication strategy among all stakeholders and, more importantly, make implementation a responsibility of all participants to the negotiation. In short, in public administration, "implementation" is everything!

The process of the Matrix of Complex Negotiation starts with preparation and then value creation. Value creation is all about:

A. Starting with the "why."
B. Starting with the price.
C. Starting with the concession.
D. Starting with the product.

The value distribution step comes:

A. After the implementation step.
B. Before the preparation step.
C. After the value creation step.
D. After the preparation step.

The value distribution step is a moment to:

A. Create options without commitment.
B. Use standards to justify price or commitment.
C. Build a relationship.
D. Talk about context.

The value creation step is about:

A. Brainstorming without criticism to look for viable solutions.
B. Bargaining about the concessions.
C. Talking about compliance with law.
D. Talking about specific standards.

The value creation is about:

A. Showing your power to impress the other.
B. Framing the problem and interests in collaboration with the other.
C. Imposing deadlines.

D. Defining penalties if the other does not respect the agreement.

The implementation step is about:

A. Carrying out the agreement.
B. Building a relationship.
C. Reducing the gap of perception.
D. Justifying the price with standards.

The interest element in our 4-10-10 technique is about:

A. Defining preferences, desires, goals, necessities of each participant.
B. Firmly advocating your position.
C. Anchoring the price and asking the other to reveal their price.
D. Hiding all your interests and keeping them for yourself.

The option element:

A. Is about the invention of possibilities, which match each interest discussed.
B. Means that you have an alternative if you do not close a deal as is.
C. Means price and nothing else.
D. Is unpleasant and full of tension.

Compliance is:

A. Due diligence to verify that all information is accurate.
B. About respecting the authority of the most powerful negotiator.
C. Is about the margin of negotiation within the bounds of the law.
D. Is about being nice.

The context element is about:

A. Analyzing the historic, economic, social, political and geographic aspects of the deal.

B. Finding an excuse to facilitate or delay the deal.

C. Showing your family background.

D. Making a diagnosis of the mental health of your opponent.

The communication/cognition element is instrumental in:

A. Making the other feel that you are smarter.

B. Revealing the weaknesses of the other.

C. Reducing the gap of perception between different negotiators.

D. Increasing the power of persuasion.

The Power element in newgotiation is destructive when it involves:

A. Avoidance of conflict.

B. Sex, money or ego.

C. Image in media.

D. Institutional relationships.

10 indicators

Satisfaction and Optimization
Rationality of decision
Emotion
Ethics/Fairness
Justice/Legal Compliance
Productivity
Social Responsibility/Environmental Sustainability
Control and Execution
Adaptability for post settlement
Technical Standards

GOTIATION INNOVATIONS IN NEGOTIATION

Figure 7.1

CHAPTER 7:
EVALUATION OF THE COMPLETED NEWGOTIATION

"Most people spend more time and energy going around problems than in trying to solve them."

Henry Ford

Our Newgotiation paradigm has no value if we are unable to implement what we negotiated or to learn from the entire process. These indicators are used to evaluate an entire agreement and perhaps more importantly its implementation. This step has intrinsic intra and extra organizational value for a sustainable relationship. Especially for our Public Administration Professionals, trust and relationships are too valuable to waste. Most of our Public Administration Professionals do not negotiate for one deal, but a series of deals and often with the same stakeholders. So, we created 10 step criteria to also evaluate our negotiation process and complete our 4-10-10 technique for newgotiation.

1. Satisfaction and Optimization. Concluding or closing a deal is already success given that only 30% of all negotiations conclude in a deal. Our Newgotiation paradigm exponentially improves this percentage but we are always looking for better. Therefore, we ask ourselves are we happy or satisfied to close this deal? Is this a full win/win? Is each step productive now or in the future? Are there any regrets? What could we have done to optimize each step? Was more preparation necessary? How about more data? Or more or different experts? Did we miss any stakeholders? Or failed to evaluate their Stakeholdership properly? Is it perhaps the undervalued BATNA? Is it the move too quickly to value distribution? Was more time necessary for implementation? Only a full assessment of our process can optimize results for this and future relationships in public sector Newgotiations.

2. Rationality of decision. Is the outcome of this negotiation rational? Did options correlate to interests? Did we solve the problems we heard from participants? Are there unintended consequences that may need adjustments in implementation? How can we mitigate unintended consequences for the future?

3. Emotion. How do we feel at the end of this negotiation? Are there still destructive emotions as a result of the long and arduous process of value distribution? Did one side concede much more than the other creating a deal and emotional imbalance? Are we still liked or respected post-closing? What is our reputation likely to be after this negotiation? How would we feel in their position? And more importantly will we return for another deal? Public Administration Professionals do not have the luxury of picking up and leaving to another market or community. They must forge a relationship that lasts. More importantly they must be credible negotiators to be able to establish a brand, a reputation to be trusted today and tomorrow.

4. Ethics/Fairness. How did we deal with self-interest? Did anyone lie or mislead? Were we fair all around? Were our solutions indiscriminate? Did we deal with each other with respect and sense of fairness? Did we use stereotypes? Did we build trust and integrity to create a good reputation for another deal?

5. Justice/Legal Compliance. Was the deal just? Was there any risk in not adhering to the rule of law? Did everyone have authority or legitimacy? Did we promise anything that we could not legally deliver? Did we open ourselves to legal liability? Is there any risk of post agreement lawsuits? Are the lawyers satisfied? What is our legal plan going forward? A word of caution here that not everything legal is just and not everything just is necessarily legal. Raising pharmaceutical prices may be legal, but is it just to a financially vulnerable community who may need the drug? Protesting during the civil rights movement may have been in violation of law, but no one will claim that such protest was not just.

6. Productivity. Were we productive given the time allocation? What is the average speed of a similar deal? Were we too fast or slow? What could we have done to improve our productivity? Companies like Pfizer have managed improving productivity by 25% by just improving collaboration between departments and sound practices of ergonomics. Others used technology to improve their processes like the city of Palo Alto or New Orleans in land use decisions or implementations. This is an area of continued opportunity in the public sector by using data and analytics.

7. Social Responsibility/Environmental Sustainability. How will this negotiation impact the community or the organization in five or ten years? What will be the impact on public policy or administration? Are our outcomes sustainable? Are we good stewards of the environment? Are we being responsible with future generations? Are we creating sources of prosperity and development based on demographic changes? Millennials are good facilitators and consumers of all these responsibilities. Did we incorporate the youth in our decisions? A well-balanced approach here incorporating economic action, community action and environmental action is what we are seeking in this criterion. The World Commission on Environment and Development at the United Nations defined this as "development that meets the needs of the present without compromising the ability of future generations to meet their own needs." Sustainable development has emerged in fact as the guiding principle for long-term global development.

8. Control and Execution. Once the negotiation is complete, the legal document or contract is signed. The next question is there operational readiness to start the implementation? Are we sure that what has been said or agreed to will be done? Is there any consequence for delay? Should there have been more consequences? Is there a penalty in case of a late payment or late delivery of product or services? Or is there a bonus for early delivery? Is there a confidentiality clause to protect intellectual property? And is there an appropriate penalty in the case of unauthorized disclosure. Are we sure that the project is fully funded? Is there a stakeholder missing, that can stop the project?

9. Adaptability for post settlement. In case of change in a currency rate for example, is there a clause to mitigate the risk of conflict? Are all the expectations included in the contract? In case one of the parties dies or files for bankruptcy how do we deal with such eventuality? Are there letters of credits or performance bonds? Does the contract contain a mechanism of naming a mediator in case of a conflict? In case the mediator does not solve the dispute, is there an arbitration clause? Which country or state will have jurisdiction to hear the matter in the case of litigation? Is there insurance covering the implementation or lack thereof? Is there a mechanism of supervision to ensure success for the long term? The management of expectations is one of the best means to prevent conflicts. Learning from and practicing these good measures will make us accomplished Newgotiators.

10. Technical Standards. Were our experts correct on the technical standards? Here we are discussing technical standards such as generally accepted accounting principles (GAAP) or American Society of Mechanical Engineers (ASME) or European Commission minimum standards for public consultations to name a few. Did we evaluate them correctly? Did we take into account possible changes in law or regulations about the technical standards? Technical data assures the customizations of options. Did we meet the expectations of the parties with technical requirements? Is there a supply of technically required parts? Is future purchasing facilitated by the technical standards in the contract? Do we have a competitive advantage here? Is risk managed? Most companies make money by buying well and mitigating risk. For example, Exxon-Mobil, the largest oil company and the third largest company in the world, creates value by cautiously reducing cost and by the proper evaluation of risk it manages. The art of negotiation is about respecting technical standards, mitigating risks and using experts to realize better value every time.

KNOWLEDGE CHECK:

The Implementation step is about

    A. Carrying out the agreement.
    B. Building a relationship.
    C. Reducing the gap of perception.
    D. Justifying the price with standards.

CHAPTER 8:
NEWGOTIATION IN PRACTICE

"Most people do not listen with the intent to understand; they listen with the intent to reply."

Stephen R. Covey

Newgotiation is a mindset to assess the challenges and opportunities available to the negotiating parties. It is a culture of collective learning to cut a better deal. Every organization can leap to greatness through collaboration, which we describe in this book as the win/win approach or frame as opposed to competition, which yields precisely the outcome it is structured to yield by one party wining and the other losing.

Competition is good for a better price or product innovation but never as a guiding principal at the outset of any negotiation.

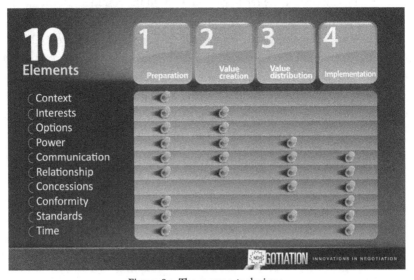

Figure 8.1: The 4-10-10 technique.

Competition at the outset destroys or even bypasses our most important value creation step in our four-step process of Newgotiation. To illustrate our entire Newgotiation 4-10-10 technique we provide the following guidance to start the conversation for our Public Administration Professionals taking our process through each step in the charts below. By no means is this guide or its questions exhaustive or complete. Each negotiation is unique and is sure to generate its own unique set of questions for each step and element we enumerate below.

Step 1: Preparation

We start by evaluating the context in which we are conducting our Newgotiation. So, for example, if the deal is about a new storm water project, the first questions are: Why are we negotiating? Is this new storm water project to benefit the entire community or even the region? Who is negotiating? Who do we need? Do we know them? If the project involves the region can we bring our neighboring cities into the discussion? How do they fit in the "why"? What is the environment like? What is the condition of the existing storm drain infrastructure? Where do we negotiate? Is our city or the neighboring city the right locality? What are the pros/cons? Is there a cost to benefit analysis available?

Next in this step and in our hypothetical storm water project example is the review of interests. What are our interests and what about the interests of our neighboring city? What about the interests of the region? What about the interests of other cities in the region? What about the interests of our constituents, groups, stakeholders or special interests? Which interests are shared and which are in conflict? What can we do or whom can we engage to resolve conflicts? What about our BATNA? What about theirs? How do we intend to use our BATNA?

What about options to solve some of the problems identified in the interests? What might satisfy the neighboring city, all other cities or the region as a whole? Can collaboration add value? What are the benefits to each participant to the Newgotiation? Is there an option that unites us as opposed to divides us? Or is there a common mission? Collaboration is a voluntary process so what are the incentives of each participant? In our hypothetical, is it the common mission to comply with water quality mandates? Or is it about a better price for all? This is the element where options are created to address various interests. Creativity and thinking differently add value for the purpose of distributing value later.

How do we minimize the negative effects of power of money, ego, manipulation and misrepresentation? Do we need a facilitator with social capital? How do we forge trust, integrity, elegance and ethics keeping in mind the "why" of the water project? Here the crucial distinction from any other sector, the public-sector negotiator considers the benefits of all his constituents and not just some special interests. In fashioning solutions to problems in his community, Frank routinely says, "I am elected to represent all the residents in my community, not just the ones discussing the problem in our council chambers." At the exception of very large cities, thankfully the power of politics or special interests plays a very small role in municipal public administration in California.

The next element is the value of communication. What have we learned in our own preparation by talking among us? How do we want to convey the importance of this water project? What do we want to learn from our negotiating colleagues? Neighboring cities? How about representatives of the region? Why should they listen to us? And how can we listen better? Do we use power points or other media to communicate? Do we communicate through intermediaries? How do we resolve inevitable disagreements in our communiqués? How do we communicate and use all stakeholders as agents for change? Here the narrative is very important. The more we align interests and values the more effective our communication strategy is.

The importance of relationships is paramount. How is our relationship with our neighboring city? What about other cities or region? Which relationships matter to us and to the group negotiating? How do we envision our relationships throughout the process of this negotiation for the water project? As we previously discussed, a thorough review of stakeholders is critical. This is important because we want to know who to invite to the discussion and who to designate to create the most elegant options.

Compliance with law and the rule of law is significant to know if we even have a project that is lawful. What is the applicable law? Are there any conflicts of laws? Is the law settled? Do we have the authority to enter into the proposed agreement? What will various stakeholders argue? Do they have the authority to act? Is the subject matter legal for the public entity that we represent? Do we need a new law to facilitate our project? For example, in the negotiation to build the Governor George Deukmejian Court House, Long Beach, California, we needed a new law to facilitate the public private partnership methodology in designing, building, financing, operating and maintaining the facility. Without the new law, the state had no authority to use the methodology as it was limited to the public contracting procurement laws.

Next is the application of standards. What external criteria or standard can we use? What standards might they use? What standard should govern the substantive topic of the agreement? Are these standards credible when applied objectively? Are they widely known or accepted? Are they technical in nature requiring an expert facilitator? What standard will a judge apply in the event of litigation?

While preparing for the value distribution step, contemplating potential concessions are paramount for a higher degree of success in closing a deal. What interests and options are we willing to concede to make a deal? What might they concede? Do we have enough options so that any concession may be balanced? As we previously suggested balance in value distribution is critical for the success of any win/win frame.

The old adage of "timing is everything" is very true in our paradigm of Newgotiation. Time is also a very important element given its own complexities we discussed previously. Therefore, is our timing correct in discussing this topic? Have we spent sufficient time to prepare? Do we have sufficient time to discuss the technicalities of this water project with the appropriate experts and stakeholders to arrive at a productive agreement. And do we have sufficient time to implement?

Step 2: Value Creation

Many despise negotiation because it is too competitive and typically distributive, also known as a single-issue negotiation. In an integrative negotiation or value creating negotiation, while parities compete for values, they integrate various sources of values to cut a better deal. This is the "why" step and fundamentally important to the success or failure of the negotiation. This is the moment of creativity, innovation and description. The questions we presented above in our preparation step with respect to interests, options, power, communication and relationship all apply here. This is where listening and brainstorming without commitment really matters. The better the value to all participants in our example of the storm water project across several jurisdictions, the better the options for possible distribution in our next step of negotiation. Of course, balanced distribution of value significantly improves the outcome. Value creation occurs best when we capitalize on differences to create opportunities, when we ask and share questions and negotiate multiple issues simultaneously.

Step 3: Value Distribution

In this step, all interests that have been explored and all options that have been invented in the previous step are ready to be committed. This is where we expose and justify our marker or price through fair and reciprocal concessions of options based on interests. In our storm water project example, the establishment of project price and the formula perhaps for payment by each city involved in the region. This step is theoretically at odds with our previous step of value creation but with sufficient options we overcome any unfair distribution or a win/lose. Again, the questions we presented above in our preparation step with respect to the elements of power, communication, relationship, concession and standards all apply here. It is important to recognize cost and benefit tradeoffs, while always selecting the bigger picture and the value for the overall deal.

Step 4: Implementation

Once value is fairly distributed the fourth step is all about follow through or implementation. The success of our first three steps yields great results in this last step. To avoid repetition, we simply note that the same questions we presented in our preparation step discussion above with respect to communication, relationship, concession, rule of law, standards and time all apply to the implementation step.

In conclusion, Newgotiation in practice builds what we hope to be a unifying global standards and language with specific benchmarks to negotiate a better deal. Public administration has long been focused on internal administration, internal conflicts and internal solutions to those conflicts. Our paradigm and process promote the culture of sharing and collaboration for the better delivery of administration. Public, private and not for profit organizations and modern institutions are introducing these new ways of learning or negotiating completely focused on collaboration or "shared value."

We are not alone in promoting the concept of shared value. In fact, we are not surprised to read in the Harvard Business Review "the solution lies in the principle of shared value, which involves creating economic value in a way that also creates value for society by addressing its needs and challenges. Businesses must reconnect company success with social progress. Shared value is not social responsibility, philanthropy, or even sustainability, but a new way to achieve economic success."

Our Newgotiation paradigm is all about aligning interests and the sharing of value not because it projects weakness or is politically correct but because our research and practice shows that it helps us deliver the better deal. Lastly, our fourth and final step puts a great emphasis on the implementation or the follow through of the negotiated deal. Public administration around the globe fails to put equal weight on planning and implementation. The challenge of the public sector as a whole is to align short-term decision making with long-term vision prescribed with the proper execution or implementation to achieve the vision. Our Newgotiation process brings a new mind set to public administration by learning to prepare, to create, to practice, to share, to innovate and implement. This more deliberate and planned process aligns with strategic planning and leadership literatures.

KNOWLEDGE CHECK:

The value distribution step is a moment to:

- A. Create options without commitment.
- B. Use standards to justify price or commitment.
- C. Build a relationship.
- D. Talk about context.

The value creation step is a about:

- A. Brainstorming without criticism to look for viable solutions.
- B. Bargaining about the concessions.
- C. Talking about compliance with law.
- D. Talking about specific standards.

The value creation is about:

- A. Showing your power to impress the other.
- B. Framing the problem and interests in collaboration with the other.
- C. Imposing deadlines.
- D. Defining penalties if the other does not respect the agreement.

CHAPTER 9:
Role of Leadership in our Newgotiation Practice

"I suppose leadership at one time meant muscles; but today it means getting along with people."

Mahatma Gandhi

"A genuine leader is not a searcher for consensus but a molder of consensus."

Martin Luther King, Jr.

"Management is doing things right; leadership is doing the right things."

Peter Drucker

"Leadership is solving problems. The day soldiers stop bringing you their problems is the day you have stopped leading them. They have either lost confidence that you can help or concluded you do not care. Either case is a failure of leadership."

Colin Powell

We believe our Public Administration Professionals are already predisposed to execute what we attempt to convey in this book for Newgotiation. They are by enlarge original innovators trusted by their communities. They are typically elected or appointed based on their reputation and brand to do what is right. They are not simply managers but leaders. Steve Jobs once said, "management is about persuading people to do things they do not want to do, while leadership is about inspiring people to do things, they never thought they could do." General Collin Powell wrote, "leadership is the art of accomplishing more than the science of management says is possible." Not every manager is a leader. While managers are motivational, delegating, mechanical and concerned with products, leaders are inspirational, persuading, creative and concerned with people. Managers administer, accept and maintain the status quo while focusing on the "how" and "when." Leaders on the other hand, innovate, develop, challenge the process focusing on the "why" and "what." Managers do things right. Leaders inspire to do the right thing. Our Newgotiation paradigm borrows extensively from the global leadership literature and practice and more specifically from the literature of facilitative, shared and appreciative leadership.

Our late colleague Professor Bennis correctly predicted that leadership "will become an increasingly intricate process of multilateral brokerage." Our colleagues Robert and Janet Denhardt suggest that shared leadership "generates more effective solutions in a fast paced and rapidly changing world." As is the case in the collaborative governance paradigm, today's complex problems require more than one sector or a manager to effectively address or solve them. We need leaders and leadership to create and distribute value. Leaders come in all sizes, shapes colors, religions and gender. Leadership is self-made. In fact, most leaders are made by circumstances and are born from challenges and not from a particular family or even born in royalty. Warren Bennis famously said "the most dangerous leadership myth is that leaders are born-that there is a genetic factor to leadership. This myth asserts that people simply either have certain charismatic qualities or not. That's nonsense: in fact, the opposite is true. Leaders are made rather than born." While we train people to be managers, we develop leaders by giving them the tools to help themselves and to rise to the challenge of leadership.

Diane Whitney, the author of the book Appreciative Leadership in a short essay wrote, "The five practices of appreciative leadership are highly congruent with successful participatory planning. They can be summarized as: inclusion, inquiry, illumination, inspiration and integrity." Dr. Whitney in her book promotes "inclusive dialogue among stakeholders, collaborative inquiry and participatory planning" all notions that we embrace in our Newgotiation paradigm. Our preparation and value creation steps rely on our negotiators ability to identify stakeholders, promote dialogue, integration and collaboration.

James MacGregor Burns' Pulitzer Prize-winning book, "Leadership," conceptualized leadership in terms of values and transformation. The growing interest in leadership literature moved from featuring "power" at the center to the importance of "purpose" or as we previously articulated in our preparation and value creation steps of Newgotiation as the "why." Burns argues that the central element in the relationship between leaders and followers is, in fact purpose. Leaders succeed when their purpose aligns with the purpose of their followers. Good leaders and Newgotiators describe the "why" so eloquently that people in fact follow or align.

When we asked our colleague and mentor, Professor Chet Newland, former policy advisor to President Lyndon B. Johnson, what do successful leaders do most? He said, "Get help and give help." Get help from subject matter experts, policy experts and "leaders" in their own rights. Then give help through exemplary leadership by "modeling the way," inspiring, challenging, enabling and encouraging others.

We think that our prototypes of Newgotiators are successful leaders. They get help by experts and staff by establishing principles and parameters concerning the way constituents, peers, colleagues and customers are expected to be treated. They give help by creating standards of excellence and setting an example for others to follow. They envision the future by creating an ideal and unique image of what it can be. They give help by innovating and challenging the status quo.

Leadership is beyond authority. A good leader provides a guiding vision with hope, passion, integrity, curiosity and is not afraid of taking risks. Robert Kennedy said, "only those who dare to fail greatly can ever achieve greatly." Finally, the famous race car driver Mario Andretti summed it up best "if things seem under control, you are just not going fast enough."

We implore our public leader Newgotiators to engage, listen, take calculated risks, discern and act with rigor, discipline, accountability and transparency for everyone to win. We ask them to collaborate with mutual respect to sustain extraordinary efforts creating trust and human dignity. We encourage them to share rewards of collaborative efforts to celebrate accomplishments. The pedagogy of sustainable leadership is consistent with our 10 elements in our technique. Leaders possess context awareness, interest recognition, value creation with options. They use reasonable power to communicate and forge lasting relationships built on trust. We note that several books have been written on these topics including the popular book by Steven R. Covey on the habits of effective people in leadership.

If our readers here recognize our prior descriptions of facilitators and visionaries, it is not by coincidence. It is also not a coincidence to observe that these characteristics of leaders enlighten our four-step process and perfectly set up Newgotiation. Finally, it is not a coincidence that Newgotiation Elements 5 ("communication") and 6 ("relationship,") are applicable to all four steps of our Newgotiation technique and are anchored by these characteristics including visioning, listening, innovating and building trust.

We previously discussed the role of collaborative governance in the 21st century. By necessity and temperament our future leaders, Millennials, are already making decisions through collaboration. Intra and inter sectoral partnerships are being forged to deliver a better and more efficient product or service. All this while diversity of perspectives, culture and talent are expanding. To achieve better results with collaboration, facilitators and visionaries are replacing authoritarians and controllers.

The essence of facilitative leadership is a skill set already familiar to our Newgotiators and Public Administration Professionals. For example, successful Newgotiators and Public Administration Professionals already actively listen, paraphrase, summarize, reflect and question to encourage and generate participative discussions with their constituents. They ask more powerful and strategic questions to stimulate creative thinking through brainstorming in public meetings organized to achieve a wide range of goals and objectives. These are skills necessary to create value.

We find many successful examples of such meetings in the public domain with what many call a "first look" to a project to evaluate the possibilities. Examples include a "charrette" or "first look" at a future municipal budget or land use entitlements for a project or even town hall meetings to shape policy. Newgotiators and Public Administration Professionals as facilitators already consider alternatives, contrasting perspectives and opinions for informed decision making because they know that collective capacity building not only encourages learning together but also betters collective decision-making. Again, this mirrors our value creation and value distribution steps of our Newgotiation paradigm.

Public and facilitative leaders provide direction without controlling the way. They are convinced that each person participating to the dialogue is holding a piece of the puzzle. Public Administration Professionals are committed to collectively shaping the "why" knowing that it improves buy-in from their constituents and substantially improves chances of persuasive value creation and value distribution for the community at large. Without a doubt, the skills of a facilitative leader provide wonderful tools to practice our 4-10-10 Newgotiation technique.

Dr. Whitney in her book "Appreciative Leadership" defines it as "a philosophy, a way of being and a set of strategies that give rise to practices applicable across industries, sectors and arenas of collaborative action." She discusses the power of being positive "to set in motion positive ripples of confidence, energy, enthusiasm and performance-to make a positive difference in the world." Our four-step process precisely contemplates the power of the positive to anchor a better outcome. Through positive relationships, conversations, inclusions and collaborations we are able to achieve the true meaning of the "why" for all participants, which leads to better and more fruitful Newgotiations.

Our late colleague Warren Bennis wrote, "Leadership is the capacity to translate vision into reality." The French observer Alexis de Tocqueville noted more than 160 years ago, "Americans seem to have a genius for collective action." Judging from history neither were wrong. Stephen Covey called this habit, "inspire a shared vision." Leaders passionately believe that they can make a difference. They envision the future, creating an ideal and singular image of what we can become. They breathe life into their visions to make us see the possibilities. Through their magnetism and use of simple metaphors, leaders enlist others to participate to their dreams. Martin Luther Ling, Jr. in his August 28, 1963 "I have a dream" speech illustrates this point very well.

"In a sense, we've come to our nation's capital to cash a check. When the architects of our republic wrote the magnificent words of the Constitution and the Declaration of Independence, they were signing a promissory note to which every American was to fall heir. This note was a promise that all men, yes, black men as well as white men, would be guaranteed the "unalienable Rights" of "Life, Liberty and the pursuit of Happiness." It is obvious today that America has defaulted on this promissory note, insofar as her citizens of color are concerned. Instead of honoring this sacred obligation, America has given the Negro people a bad check, a check which has come back marked "insufficient funds."

But we refuse to believe that the bank of justice is bankrupt. We refuse to believe that there are insufficient funds in the great vaults of opportunity of this nation. And so, we've come to cash this check, a check that will give us upon demand the riches of freedom and the security of justice."

The simplicity of moral bankruptcy and a bad check as a concept gave rise to the debate on race discrimination. King's dream was shared by the American people, who supported and passed the Civil Rights Act of 1964.

All visions as projects "that put a dent in the universe" according to Steve Jobs were realized through leadership and collective action or collaborations such as Macintosh (Apple), Disney in the creation of Mickey and Mini and friends, The Manhattan Project with the production of the atomic bomb, Hewlett Packard (HP) and Star Wars the movie. These are not mere flukes. The culture and style of our Newgotiator is precisely based on collaboration, shared values, experiences and shared learning.

Our Newgotiators as facilitators and curators create opportunities for people to come together. They promote holistic, systemic, connective and ecological ways of developing and learning together. They are open to change but they tie change to their core values.

We expect nothing less from our Public Administration Professionals today. We are reminded by the lessons of a pastor leading his congregation in a demographically transitioning neighborhood. Elders of the congregation fearing the new ethnic mix, pushed back on change and on the admission of new members to the church. When asked the question, "pastor why we should accept new members who are ethnically diverse from us?" the pastor thinking like a true leader and Newgotiator responded by asking three questions to be able to frame his response (it is all about the frame). First, he said, "what does the New Testament say about the Christian faith and race relations?" "what would Jesus say about the matter" and "is this his church or yours?" The Pastor's questions clearly reveal his ability to lead change through core values. In this instance, the core values of his and the congregation's Christian faith.

We both teach in executive programs designed for first responders as well as military officers. Frank teaches regularly at the Ministry of Defense and Military Universities of the Republic of Armenia. There we emphasize change through values, especially given that these organizations pride themselves as value driven organizations. Shared interests and values are the hallmark of these organizations.

The United States Army teaches leadership by separating attributes of leadership from competencies of leadership. The first attribute of a leader topping the chart is character. The Army defines character as, "Army values," empathy, service, discipline and "warrior ethos." We discuss in our Newgotiation paradigm the importance of empathy, service and value driven collaboration to cut a better deal. The second attribute values the presence of a military officer including her fitness, confidence and resilience. Intellect, or mental agility, judgment and expertise represents the third attribute of a leader. We use all these attributes in our Newgotiation process.

The competencies described by the Army include leadership, development and achievement. Not much different than preparation, value creation, value distribution and implementation. Leadership by leading others, building trust, extending influence, leading by example and through effective communication. Development is expected by every officer in terms of self-development as well as the development of others through the creation of positive environments. Achievement is about implementation, getting results, integrating tasks, roles, resources and priorities. More importantly, it is about learning to fail to only do it over again and better.

Among others, Newgotiation extensively borrows from the literatures of:

A. Mathematics and physics.
B. Collaborative governance and leadership.
C. Reptilian Brian Science.
D. English literature.

Shared leadership generates:

A. More problems than it is worth.
B. Pricey products and services.
C. More effective solutions in a rapidly changing world.
D. Soft solutions.

Good leaders:

A. Do not concern themselves with small problems.
B. Promote their own views.
C. Give help by creating standards of excellence and setting an example for others to follow.
D. Are egomaniacs.

Our goal is...

Newgotiation

INNOVATIONS IN NEGOTIATION

"You can observe a lot by just watching."

Yogi Berra

Our 4-10-10 Newgotiation technique is a place to test options, analyze the context, make concessions, improve relationships, manage power, reduce misunderstandings, respect rules, determine norms and manage time. Our 4-10-10 Newgotiation technique is a unified dialect, which helps organizations to speak the same language of Newgotiation. Our Newgotiation paradigm is both strategic and tactical. Leaders tend to be strategic and managers tactical. Strategy is about the big picture. It is comprehensive, mission driven, broad and innovative. This is what we described in our preparation and value creation steps of Newgotiation. Strategy aligns the thinking of various stakeholders involved. It provides a framework for action, unleashing energy towards a shared vision through core values. Strategy clarifies the mission or the purpose or the "why" with unambiguous communication. It sets goals and accountability for stakeholders and negotiators. Tactics on the other hand are the more specific details of the deal like conformity, standards, time and generally implementation as a step. Tactics are task driven, narrow, more granular in scope to improve operations and methods. Our paradigm of Newgotiation needs both. The Chinese military leader and philosopher Sun Tzu, who is credited with "The Art of War" captures this well, "strategy without tactics is the slowest route to victory. Tactics without strategy is the noise before defeat."

When all organizations, public and private, practice Newgotiation, the relationships between all sectors and even between all levels of governments improve dramatically yielding better and sustainable results through trust. Hillary Clinton revealed in her book that traditionally the State Department barely communicated with the Defense Department of the United States. This tradition of poor communication, lack of collaboration and strategic planning exposed some of the most serious foreign policy blunders of modern times. Rigidity by each department in silo like environments creates inhibition and clear inefficiencies in public administration.

A more contemporary challenge in this context is the emergence of various uncompromising positions about various viewpoints. Adding politics to this mix creates the polarization that we experience in the United States as well as around the world. An interest-based discussion will always be more productive than a position-based discussion. For example, the Climate Change debate is purportedly framed between believers and non-believers. Those who believe in the rise of earth's temperature blaming humanity for most if not all global warming and those who look for a broader and more natural culpability. At the outset the frame is very competitive. Both groups seeking superiority over the other.

This debate escalates everyday with symmetrical rivalry between the various and politically motivated organizations. Unfortunately, public administration and economic development take a back seat to the name-calling. The debate needs an "Ambassador Talleyrand" to change the narrative to a more productive one. We do need to address climate change at the most local level to be impactful. More importantly we need collaboration rather than competition. President Macron, in his speech to US Congress said, "I believe in building a better future for our children, which requires offering them a planet that is still habitable in 25 years." Does anyone disagree with this statement?

Skilled negotiators instead of fueling political fires ask what if we were to invent a more creative and graceful option or narrative in discussing the role and responsibility of each sector and organization in environmental stewardship to preserve the natural resources of the earth that we all share? Each sector (public, private and not for profit) bears responsibility in this endeavor. They can all contribute with real solutions.

Our anecdotal research in discussing climate change with both sides of the debate found that no one enjoys drinking from a polluted river or ground water; no one enjoys swimming in an oil spill or breath from the exhaust pipe of a diesel truck. Newgotiators focus on what unites us before highlighting what divides us. Skipping preparation and value creation steps of our technique are fatal to any negotiation. This debate has become all or nothing and a zero-sum game. A very competitive frame to continue to create winners and losers.

Instead of competing for climate change can we collaborate based on a common mission? Ironically, the so called "deniers" that we listened to with an open mind and empathetic ear could care much less on the warming or the cause of the debate rather than the fear of the unknown or what they say the "fear of big government" solutions proposed to curtail the warming or the uneven application of regulations displacing economic development from one country to the next willing country in the same globe. Both sides of the debate fear without any alignment.

The important question is whether we can reframe the debate to prepare and create value in our Newgotiation paradigm by bringing in all stakeholders to frame multi-dimensional and multi sectoral solutions to save the earth for future generations? A healthy debate on these solutions in our value distribution step will advance this debate positively as opposed to the nonproductive name calling, we continue to experience by both sides.

While it is not our subject matter expertise to take this climate change debate through our 4-10-10 Technique substantively, we can clearly see a path through the process. Our Newgotiation paradigm and technique promotes a vision of horizontal and systemic approach to sharing in order to create value to be able to distribute value. Yann calls this "breaking the eggs to make an omelet."

We are not alone in promoting sharing or collaboration. Robert D. Putnam in "Bowling Alone" explains how some public-school reduced bicycle accidents around campus by 30% by simply sharing information between parents, teachers, bicycle manufacturers, urban planners, police officers and trauma surgeons. Pfizer improved productivity by simply taking out walls in their offices to connect their employees promoting natural sharing and collaboration. Google instituted interdepartmental networking days. Microsoft created social gathering places like coffee stores on campus to promote informal meetings and collaboration between its employees.

Newgotiation is a technique that can be taught. Having taught and practiced what we preach, we firmly believe that everyone can be a good negotiator armed with the same lexicon of ingredients that we discuss in this book. We are convinced that the methodic application of our 4-10-10 Newgotiation Technique is the way for the future advancement of this art and science that we call Newgotiation. Remember it is all about the frame!

We leave you with a story and reflection of unknown origins but quite impactful to the behavior of the Newgotiator.

A Cherokee elder sitting with his grandchildren in a teaching moment said, "In every life there is a terrible fight - -a fight between two wolves. One is evil: he is fear, anger, envy, greed, arrogance, self-pity, resentment and deceit. The other is good: joy, serenity, humility, confidence, generosity, truth, gentleness, and compassion."

A child asked, "Grandfather, which wolf will win?" The elder looked him in the eye and with a pleasant smile said,

"The one you feed."

BIBLIOGRAPHY

A. Abbas E. 2018. Foundations of Multiattribute Utility. Cambridge University Press. Forthcoming.

A. Damasio. The Feeling of What Happens: Body and Emotion in the Making of Consciousness, Harcourt, 1999

A. Lempereur, A. Colson, Y. Duzert org. Metodo de Negociação. Editora Atlas. 2008

A. Levitt and Waren Buffett. Take on the Street, What Wall Street and Corporate America Don't Want You to Know. Pantheon. 2002.

A. Sen. Ethics and Economy. Oxford Publishing. 1988.

B. Cavalcanti, Y. Duzert, E. Marques. Guerreiro Ramos. Editora FGV. 2014.

B. Clinton. Giving. Knopf Publishing.

B. Nalebuff and A. Brandenburger. Competition. Currency Doubleplay. 1997

D. Goleman. Focus, The Hidden Driver of Excellence. Harper Collins. 2013.

D. Goleman. Gentle Bridges. Shambhala Publications. 2001

D. Goleman. The Brain and Emotional Intelligence. Batham books. 2014

David Lax & James Sebenius. 3-D Negotiation: Powerful Tools to Change the Game in Your Most Important Deals. Harvard University Press. 2011

D. Whitney. Appreciative Leadership. McGraw Hill. 2010

E. Schmitt. Nova Era Digital. Knopf Publishing. 2013

F. Saltman. Votre Meilleur Remède c'est Vous. Albin Michel. 2013

F. Varela. Embodied Mind. MIT Press

F. Zerunyan and P. Pirnejad. From Contract Cities to Mass Collaborative Governance. American City & County. April 2014

F. Zerunyan and Tatevik Sargsyan. Analysis of Legislative and Institutional Frameworks of Ethical Regulation in the Public Service System. Public Administration Scientific Journal Republic of Armenia. June and December 2016

G. Cavalcanti. Decolando Para o Futuro. 2012

G. Klein. Sources of Power. How People Make Decisions. MIT Press. 1999

Guhan Subramanian. The New Strategy of Negotiations.

H. Movius and L. Susskind. Built to Win. Harvard University Press. 2009

H. Raiffa. Negotiation Analysis: The Science and Art of Collaborative Decision. 2004

H. Raiffa. The Art and Science of Negotiation. Harvard University Press. 1993

H. Simon. Models of Bound Rationality. MIT Press.

H. Simon. Models of Bounded Rationality. MIT Press. 1997

Ingrid Paola Stoeckicht, Dorval Olivio Mallman, João C. Men, Yann Duzert. Negociação internacional. Editora FGV. 2014

J. Attali. Urgence Francaise. Editions Fayard. 2014.

J. Casablancas. Vida Modelo. Agir. 2008

J. Gray. Man are From Mars and Women from Venus. HarperCollins. 2004.

J. MacGregor Burns. Leadership. Harper Perennial Political Classics. 2010

J. Sebenius and Lax. The Manager as Negotiator. Free Press. 2011.

J. Sebenius, A. Lempereur. Y. Duzert. Manual de Negociações Complexas. Editora FGV. 2004.

J. von Neumann, and O. Morgenstern. 1947. Theory of games and economic behavior, 2nd ed. Princeton, NJ: Princeton University Press

J. Welsh. Straight from the Gut. Business Plus. 2003

J. Welsh. Winning. Harper Collins. 2013

J.P. Dupuy On the Origins of Cognitive Science: The Mechanization of the Mind. MIT Press. 2009.

K. Arrow, R. Mnookin, L. Ross, A. Tversky, Y. Duzert. Obstaculos Para Resolução de Conflitos. Editora FGV/Saraiva. 2007.

L. Susskind, Y Duzert, A. Lempereur. Faciliter la Concertation. Editions Eyrolles. 2010.

L. Susskind, Y. Duzert. J. Cruickshank. Quando a Maioria Não Basta. Editora FGV. 2008.

L. Susskind. Good for You, Great for Me. Public Affairs. 2014.

M. Bazerman. Predictable Surprise. Perseus Publishing. 2008.

M. Bazerman. With Technical Revision Yann Duzert. Processo Decisório. Editora Campus. 2014

M. Hardt and A. Negri. Empire. Harvard University Press. 2000.

M. Mobius Passport to profit. Grand Central Publishing. 2000.

M. Naim. The End of Power. Basic books. 2013

M. Seligman. Authentic Happiness. Atria Books. 2004

M. Wheeler. The Art of Negotiation: How to Improvise Agreement in a Chaotic World. Simon & Shuster. 2014.

M. Wheeler. What is Fair. Ethics for Negotiators. Jossey Bass. 2004

N. Berggruen. Smart Governance for the XXI Century. Polity. 2012

Nassim Nicholas Taleb. Black Swan, The Impact of Highly Improbable. Random House. 2010.

R. Bellino. You Have 3 Minutes. McGrawHill. 2006

R. Cialdini. The Power of Persuasion. Harper Collins. 2013.

R. Mnookin. Negotiating with the Devil. When to Fight and When to Negotiate. Simon & Schuster. 2011

R. Howard, A and A. E. Abbas. 2015. Foundations of Decision Analysis, Pearson, NY, NY.

R. Putnam. Bowling Alone. Simon & Schuster. 2001

R. Reich. Supercapitalism. Knopf Doubleplay. 2007

S. Covey. Seven Habits of Highly Effective People. Free Press. 2004

S. Covey. Smart Trust. Simon & Schuster. 2013

S. Covey. Speed of Trust. Simon & Schuster. 2006

S. Sinek. Start with Why. Penguin Book. 2009

T. Cooper. The Responsible Administrator. Jossey-Bass/Wiley, 2012

T. Shilling. Strategy of Conflict. Harvard University Press. 1960

W. Chan Kim and Renée Mauborgne Ocean

W. Ury. Getting to Past No. Random House Publishing Group. 2009

W. W. Norton & Company. 2011

Y. Duzert, A.T. Spinola. A. Brandão. Negociações empresarias. Editora Saravia. 2007

Y. Duzert, A.T. Spinola. F. Lustosa. Aprendiz Legal. Editora FRM. 2011.

This appendix contains questions posed throughout the book, as well as additional questions to test your knowledge of Newgotation. (Note: all best answers are highlighted in italic. A short explanation is provided at the bottom of each question.)

Question 1: Newgotiation is all about selective influence.

A. True. Newgotiation is about targeting the opponent to lead him/her to the select decision.
B. *False. Newgotiation is not about selective influence but a collective learning and decision-making process to score a win/win.*
C. True. Newgotiation is all about making the other believe that you are right.
D. True. Newgotiation is the art and science of imposing your values.

Answer (B): Newgotiation is an ethical and elegant process of rational and collaborative decision-making aimed at mutual benefits.

Question 2: Newgotiation is all about an integrative approach and it means:

A. *The creation of value through the invention of more than one option.*
B. The Integration of more than two stakeholders.
C. The integration of different standards.
D. The reliance on different concessions.

Answer (A): In a Newgotiation options add value and improve our ability to achieve a better deal. The more options the easier the distribution and more room for concessions in ideal deal making.

Question 3: The authoritarian as a negotiator:

A. Listens more than s/he talks.
B. Creates and makes concessions.
C. *Prefers domination to create value.*
D. Loves peace.

Answer (C): The Authoritarian is a person who sees the art of war, the games of power as the sources of contentment of his/her ego. S/he does not share and prefers the domination method to create value without ever wanting to distribute it.

Question 4: The controller:

A. Is more risk prone than risk averse.
B. *Uses norms, standards, legal framework and compliance as a source of trust.*
C. Likes to brainstorm about new ideas.
D. Trusts people.

Answer (B): The controller loves to control the situation with or without the authority. S/he hates insecurity. The virtue of people who have a sense of uncertainty and doubt is to look for norms, standards and law to validate beliefs.

Question 5: The facilitator, on the other hand:

A. Uses power tactics to lead groups.
B. *Accommodates cooperation and finds harmony.*
C. Uses time to pressure fast decisions.
D. Uses fear to make people cooperate.

Answer (B): The facilitator is a humanist with intensions to help, gather and integrate. S/he trusts people, accepts differences, conciliates at work and at home. S/he accommodates cooperation, flexibility and finds harmony.

Question 6: The visionary negotiator:

A. Makes decisions based upon principles of precaution.
B. Negotiates based upon monetary rewards.
C. Wants to be an average person.
D. *Thinks long term.*

Answer (D): The visionary thinks about time, about legacy about how he will be remembered. S/he is prepared to sacrifice him/herself for a greater cause, and for future generations. S/he thinks long term.

Question 7: The entrepreneur as a negotiator:

A. *Sees negotiation as an exploratory conversation for an unprecedented gain.*
B. Sees negotiation all about compliance with norms and law.
C. Sees negotiation all about following the best practices.
D. Sees negotiation to be about reducing costs.

Answer (A): The entrepreneur is risk prone and prefers the chance to a "jackpot." S/he wants to be the first at everything as that is where s/he can create more opportunity.

Question 8: The authoritarian negotiator cares more about:

A. Price.
B. Relationship.
C. Concessions.
D. *Having more than the other.*

Answer (D): The authoritarian fits best in a hierarchical system of governance. S/he threatens those who do not agree with him/her and rewards those who accept his/her ways and rules.

Question 9: The controller is more likely to like somebody who is:

A. *Traditional.*

B. Different.

C. Funny.

D. Creative.

Answer (A): The controller likes routines, organized best practices and proof to leave no doubt. To attract a controller one must be down to earth, responsible, logical and committed. Responsibility, education and maturity are skills that a controller prefers.

Question 10: The visionary is more likely to:

A. *Make concessions.*

B. Flee.

C. Follow standards.

D. Be impatient.

Answer (A): The visionary is even more risk prone than the entrepreneur; he is prepared to take drastic measures or make huge concessions for the good of many.

Question 11: The entrepreneur is likely to hire someone:

A. *With sparkles in his/her eyes capturing the dream of the project or company.*

B. With credentials supported by documentation, standards and benchmarks.

C. With a business plan detailed in a spreadsheet.

D. With established traditions.

Answer (A): Richard Branson in his book admitted that he looks to hire people who will sweat for the company capturing the dream. Someone who passionately loves what s/he does and demonstrates that passion through the sparkles in his/her eyes.

Question 12: To build trust with the controller:

A. One must like brainstorming to create many options.

B. One must be creative.

C. *One must show him/her proven standards and neutral data.*

D. One must tell him that s/he can be trusted.

Answer (C): The controller is not a dreamer; s/he is not a romantic; hardly an entrepreneur. S/he must have data, metrics, targets and measures to trust. Controllers look for purity, transparency and integrity before they trust.

Question 13: The facilitator's core value is:

A. *A democratic decision-making process with shared responsibilities.*

B. All can participate but the facilitator leader decides on behalf of the group.

C. The focus on price before any other issue.

D. Ego and power.

Answer (A): The facilitator enjoys building consensus even in diversity and adversity. The facilitator mindset is all about social networks, integration, justice, tactfulness and diplomacy.

Question 14: The facilitator:

A. *Accepts differences and the pleasure of the debate.*

B. Enjoys manipulation to manage people.

C. Finds transparency to be overrated.

D. Looks for conflicts.

Answer (A): The facilitator is stimulated by the intellectual challenge, the debate, the conversation and learning. S/he likes the challenge of ideas and does not mind changing his/her own mind to search for the truth. S/he looks for peaceful relationships and avoids conflicts. S/he searches for cooperation and partnerships.

Question 14: The process of the Matrix of Complex Negotiation starts with preparation then value creation. Value creation is all about:

A. *Starting with the "why."*

B. Starting with the price.

C. Starting with the concession.

D. Starting with the product.

Answer (A): Value creation is the definition of the "why" by identifying interests and options. This is the moment to be creative, innovative and descriptive. The value creation step is to address or suspend criticism and to invent options to solve problems.

Question 15: The value distribution step comes:

A. After the implementation step.

B. Before the preparation step.

C. *After the value creation step.*

D. After the preparation step.

Answer (C): The third step in our four-step technique is Value Distribution. This is when we describe or justify the critical moment or the price. Value Distribution is when we transform the options of each interest into reciprocal concessions. This is the time we metaphorically "divide the cake."

Question 16: The value distribution step is a moment to:

A. Create options without commitment.

B. *Use standards to justify price or commitment.*

C. Build a relationship.

D. Talk about context.

Answer (B): Having explored all interests, invented all possible options, this is the time to expose and justify our moment or price with objective standards and track record we established during preparation.

Question 17: The value creation step is about:

A. *Brainstorming without criticism to look for viable solutions.*

B. Bargaining about the concessions.

C. Talking about compliance with law.

D. Talking about specific standards.

Answer (A): The value creation step is to address or suspend criticism and to invent options to solve problems. The more we explore "what if's" the more we invent potential solutions to cut a better deal.

Question 18: The value creation is about:

A. Showing your power to impress the other.
B. *Framing the problem and interests in collaboration with the other.*
C. Imposing deadlines.
D. Defining penalties if the other does not respect the agreement.

Answer (B): Value creation is the step to build trust by brainstorming to frame problems and interests. This is the moment to build a joint dream or opportunity. The more the buy in at this step the better the chances of value distribution to satisfy everyone in the negotiation.

Question 19: The implementation step is about:

A. *Carrying out the agreement.*
B. Building a relationship.
C. Reducing the gap of perception.
D. Justifying the price with standards.

Answer (A): Implementation refers to the carrying out of the distributed options agreed to in our third step of Value Distribution. Agreement of known dimensions put in action.

Question 20: The interest element in our 4-10-10 technique is about:

A. *Defining preferences, desires, goals, necessities of each participant.*
B. Firmly advocating your position.
C. Anchoring the price and asking the other to reveal their price.
D. Hiding all your interests and keeping them for yourself.

Answer (A): Interest is our mission, vision, goals and the target we want to achieve through this collective learning process. If interest were only about price, it would be single dimensional, a one-sided definition of purpose leading to a very short win/lose bargaining process.

Question 21: The option element:

A. *Is about the invention of possibilities, which match each interest discussed*
B. Means that you have an alternative if you do not close a deal as is.
C. Means price and nothing else.
D. Is unpleasant and full of tension.

Answer (A): This element is about building a rapport, personalizing, customizing and matching interests with options for solutions. This element is about "enlarging the size of the pie" before "dividing the pie."

Question 22: Compliance is:

A. Due diligence to verify that all information is accurate.
B. About respecting the authority of the most powerful negotiator.
C. *Is about the margin of negotiation within the bounds of the law.*
D. Is about being nice.

Answer (C): Knowledge of the laws may shape legal interests for better options and solutions within the bounds of the law. By the same token the rule of law is a limitation for the contemplated negotiation as well as the expected outcome. An illegal contract is not implementable.

Question 23: Deadlines belong to the element of:

A. Power
B. *Time*
C. Context
D. Concession

Answer (B): Reasonable dates and time pressures are appropriate in each step of our Newgotiation process. That being said our Newgotiation process deserves and requires time to create value and distribute value.

Question 24: A contingency provision in a contract helps in cases of time constraints; it also:

A. *Facilitates negotiations in good Faith, sharing the risks and betting on them.*
B. Avoids indecision.
C. Allows the smartest to take advantage of the other.
D. Enables bluffing to manipulate the other.

Answer (A): There is no substitute for trust when seeking to improve the probability of closing a deal. Collaboration to close gaps and prevent conflicts is an absolute necessity in Newgotiation.

Question 24: The communication/cognition element is instrumental in:

A. Making the other feel that you are smarter.
B. Revealing the weaknesses of the other.
C. *Reducing the gap of perception between different negotiators.*
D. Increasing the power of persuasion.

Answer (C): Proper communication is all about reducing the gap between perceptions and reality so that both or all parties have accurate data or are on the "same page" to craft options to solve problems.

Question 25: Communication/cognition is useful to:

A. *Define jointly the problem.*
B. Show or share your marketing brochure.
C. Find the Money.
D. Define who is the most popular among negotiators.

Answer (A): The etymology and epistemology are key to effective communication and ultimately the success of the negotiation. Jointly defining problems forges joint problem solving which facilitates better deals.

Question 26: The context element is about:

A. *Analyzing the historic, economic, social, politic, geographic aspects of the deal.*
B. Finding an excuse to facilitate or delay the deal.
C. Showing your family background.
D. Making a diagnosis of the mental health of your opponent.

Answer (A): Context impacts the environment in which the negotiation takes place. The context analysis occurs during the preparation step of Newgotiation when parties gather information to frame the problem and describe the "why" in an elegant manner.

Question 27: Power tactic good cop, bad cop can be neutralized by:

A. Looking only at the good cop and ignoring the bad cop.
B. Convincing the bad cop of your point of view.
C. *Bringing your own bad cop with you to retaliate against this unproductive tactic.*
D. Bringing a good cop to focus on the other good cop.

Answer (C): This cooperative and competitive tactic in one is not really useful to our Newgotiation paradigm. Good preparation and the power of anticipation are good tools to avoid the tactic all together. Negotiating with someone with authority while building trust and social capital will most likely avoid the use of this tactic.

Question 28: The Zone of Possible Agreement is:

A. *Between the Price anchored by negotiator A and the price anchored by negotiator B.*
B. The neutral place for negotiations.
C. The Courthouse where a judge can rule on the agreement.

D. The moment when one wins and the other loses.

Answer (A): The difference between two price points also known as perhaps the point of compromise. More importantly ZOPA bypasses very important steps of Newgotiation; preparation and value creation. Value distribution or anchoring the price before value creation is completely counterproductive in creating the better deal.

Question 29: The best alternative to a negotiated agreement is:

A. The best solution for a negotiation.
B. *The Plan B as an available alternative in case plan A is no longer feasible.*
C. The best possible option to make a deal happen.
D. The concession you must make to arrive at a deal.

Answer (B): BATNA is our plan B in any negotiation. BATNA provides us with the power to walk away from a weak opportunity for a deal. The better the BATNA the stronger our ability to negotiate.

Question 30: The power element in newgotiation is destructive when it involves:

A. Avoidance of conflict.
B. *Sex, money or ego.*
C. Image in media.
D. Institutional relationships.

Answer (B): Self-centered motivations like sex, money and ego are major sources of corruption. They are addictive. They operate counter to any notion of collaboration we articulate in our Newgotiation paradigm.

Question 31: The limbic brain is:

A. *Primitive and instinctive.*
B. Logical and linguistic.
C. Not useful.
D. Calculated.

Answer (A): The primitive and instinctive nature of a negotiation comes from the limbic brain; it is part of the brain that our prehistoric ancestors developed before the neo-cortex. The limbic brain does not speak and is all about the 5 senses.

Question 32: The neo-cortex enables:

A. Smell and touch.
B. Aesthetics.
C. Drinking.
D. *Logic and Language.*

Answer (D): The neo-cortex is the analytic brain, which developed with vocal expression or language. We use both our limbic and neo-cortex brains in Newgotiation but for different purposes.

Question 33: The reptilian brain creates behaviors of:

A. *Envy, food, drink, obsession, having more than the other.*
B. Love and empathy.
C. Caring about the other's well-being.
D. Cowardice.

Answer (A): Most likely the oldest part of the human brain. First and foremost, among the traits generated through the reptilian brain is the drive to establish and defend territory. This is fueled by an extremely potent "will-to-power", exemplified among lizards by the ritual behavior of two rainbow lizards competing for dominance.

Question 34: Cortisol is the hormone of:

A. Serenity and positive thinking.
B. Enthusiasm and passion.
C. *Fear, risk aversion and prevention of catastrophe.*
D. Love of the unknown.

Answer (C): Cortisol is what is responsible for shutting down the immune response and increasing glucose uptake in the body when the body is threatened. It is cortisol that allows the body to prioritize running from danger as more important than repair and rejuvenation.

Question 35: The dopamine and adrenaline fuel:

A. *Passion, euphoria, fighting stress.*
B. Peace and fear of taking risks.
C. Caring and slow motion.
D. Making concessions.

Answer (A): Dopamine is most notably responsible for feelings of pleasure and euphoria. It also plays an important role in locomotion, learning, memory and other emotions. Adrenaline provides us the strength to combat stressful events.

Question 36: Oxytocin and estrogen are hormones of:

A. Confrontation and conflict.
B. Independence and indifference.
C. *Loving, caring, grace and collaboration.*
D. Hate and anger.

Answer (C): Oxytocin is sometimes referred to as the "bonding hormone". There is some evidence that oxytocin promotes ethnocentric behavior, incorporating the trust and empathy of in-groups with their suspicion and rejection of outsiders. Women are biologically advantaged here hence their ability to be predisposed to collaborate.

Question 37: Creating value in Newgotiation requires:

A. *Seeing the other more than just a customer, but a partner and agent for change.*
B. Making the customer king.
C. Yielding to customers' wants and desires.
D. Creating the best price as it is the only thing that matters.

Answer (A): Collaboration requires more than just working together. Creation of value starts with the framing of the common mission, commitment to shared values power and talent with no single entity dominating the discussion. This is where we are discussing the "why."

Question 38: Research shows that the most important reason why the client leaves his supplier is:

A. The price
B. The quality
C. The distance
D. *The relationship*

Answer (D): Social capital in the creation of human capital and building trust through relationships are the most important ingredients of our Newgotiation paradigm. People who know and trust each other forge long lasting human and commercial relationships.

Question 39: The Newgotiation framework shows that:

A. Power is conducive to a good and working relationship.
B. *Communication/Cognition improves the relationship.*
C. Stereotypes really matter because people always behave the same way.
D. Establishing targets and hitting them at all costs help long term deal making.

Answer (B): Consistent and open communications build trust and reputation. To succeed in Newgotiations we need both. Communication/Cognition is important in all four steps of Newgotiation because it helps create value, distribute value and help in the effective implementation process.

Question 40: The Newgotiation framework promotes:

A. The "take it or leave it" concept in negotiations.
B. Moral elegance and graceful ways to improve profitability.
C. Manipulation of the other.

D. Hiding feelings and bluffing.

Answer (B): Newgotiation is about setting limits, being cooperative and competitive, it is about being empathetic, soft and gentle with people but tough in
the defense of core and ethical values. It is truly a balanced moral and graceful
holistic approach to see if value can be created for greater returns.

Question 41: Power tactics are most likely to impede:

A. Decision-making.
B. *The quality of an established relationship.*
C. Motivation for a deal.
D. Zone of Possible Agreement.

Answer (B): In simple terms there is no substitute for trust, community or
social networks seeking to improve relationships, which in turn help closing the better deal. Collaboration improves productivity through sharing
and prevents conflict. Power tactics put in risk the established good will and
relationship, which takes time to build. Relationship building is an expensive
commodity. Risking this for a short-term gain is literally shortsighted.

Question 42: Communication/cognition is helpful to:

A. *Revising, re-inventing and updating beliefs.*
B. Imposing your view onto others.
C. Excluding those who do not see things your way.
D. Saying that all is relative and therefore remaining indecisive.

Answer (A): Story telling nicely correlates to this element. In our preparation
and value creation steps we brain storm through communication/cognition
revising, re-inventing and updating our beliefs so that we are able to come up
with good options to solve problems.

Question 43: Joint fact-finding helps:

A. Proving the facts that the leaders claim to be true.
B. Excluding minority views.

C. *Integrating all points of view for a better buy in by all during value distribution.*

D. Defining facts and finding experts to prove them.

Answer (C): This is the main ingredient of any collaborative process. Learning together promotes more innovation, creativity and collective understanding of framed problems to find suitable solutions. Everyone feels invested and more accepting of outcomes, which tend to be fair and balanced.

Question 44: A good Newgotiator is:

A. Someone who is focused on a target and knows how to hit it.

B. *Someone who listens and learns from the other to make an ethical, rational and collaborative decision.*

C. Someone who is able to manipulate others.

D. Someone who always has the last word.

Answer (B): Newgotiation is all about empathetic listening to align interests, create options and invent solutions. The Greek philosopher Epictetus said it best "we have two ears and one mouth so that we can listen twice as much as we speak." The overall themes of empathy and listening should not come as a surprised to our trainees.

Question 45: A facilitator is a person:

A. *Who integrates, connects and shares information to find elegant rational solutions.*

B. Who simplifies everything and excludes all people who complicate things.

C. Who creates deadlines to put pressures for a faster deal.

D. Who is a weak consensus builder.

Answer (A): The facilitator is stimulated by the intellectual challenge, the debate, the conversation and learning. S/he looks for peaceful relationships and avoids conflicts. S/he searches for cooperation and partnerships through sharing, networking and diplomacy.

Question 46: A newgotiator:

A. *Works to redistribute power and control from a central authority to many vested actors.*
B. Creates departmental boundaries and limits interaction.
C. Believes that a company or an organization is only a vertical hierarchy.
D. Hires people who agree with him/her.

Answer (A): Groups practicing intersectoral collaboration, work to redistribute power and control to innovate, cooperate, coordinate to transact the better deal. The Newgotiator promotes transparency, efficiency, effectiveness, participation, accountability and results.

Question 47: Newgotiation is best supported by technology that:

A. Allows to monitor people.
B. *Allows a person to share and resolve conflicts collectively.*
C. Helps find a person a single solution to a problem.
D. Hinders interpersonal relationships for a personal gain.

Answer (B): Technology is necessary to communicate. Communication is an important element at all stages (steps) of Newgotiation. Anything to lubricate collective decision-making is a welcome opportunity for Newgotiation.

Question 48: Cross-cultural negotiations are best resolved:

A. When people negotiate just by email and never meet in person.
B. When people clearly state their own cultural norms.
C. *When people avoid stereotyping and consider all cultural norms.*
D. When people establish that culture equals wealth.

Answer (C): The impact of culture on negotiation is significant. We are different in the global community and east does not necessarily means west. This is not one size fits all and stereotyping impedes our ability to be on the same page to collaborate.

Question 49: Concessions in Value Distribution are desirable:

A. *When equal or near equal number of options are available to all.*
B. When they are limited.
C. When they highlight a weakness.
D. When they are a pain and never a pleasure.

Answer (A): The moment of value distribution is when we transform the options of each into reciprocal concessions. This is the time when we "divide the cake" however the larger the cake the more opportunity to divide and distribute value. Single options or uneven options never promote a good Newgotiation outcome.

Question 50: Trust in negotiation is built:

A. *With fair standards and criteria, which show objectivity and good faith.*
B. By the use of body language to impress the other.
C. By simply asking the other to trust you.
D. Payment of a large sum of money.

Answer (A): The art and science of negotiation emphasizes the importance of building trust, common purpose and belief systems. To this with credibility, fair and objective standards are used in good faith.

Question 51: "Game Theory" in the negotiation context is when:

A. Negotiators bluff or hide their knowledge.
B. *Negotiators coordinate their strategy for mutual benefit.*
C. Negotiators make concessions without any demand for reciprocity.
D. Negotiators claim satisfaction when everyone loses.

Answer (B): Game Theory is taught or used in the negotiation context to highlight the effectiveness of a coordinated response to a dilemma. This is also sometime referred to as the prisoners' dilemma.

Question 52: Moral elegance is all about:

    A. *Treating people with civility, dignity, kindness and empathy.*
    B. Having elegant clothes, smelling good and driving a nice car.
    C. Judging people based on their socioeconomic status.
    D. Respecting the authority of leaders.

Answer (A): Moral elegance is all about our humanity. It has nothing to do with materiality or socioeconomic status. It includes life skills like empathy, ethics, passion, vision, respect and fairness.

Question 53: Newgotiation:

    A. Improves the probability to make a deal by anchoring the price first.
    B. Improves the probability to make a deal by exerting more power.
    C. Improves the probability to make a deal by hiding interests or motivations.
    D. *Improves the probability to make a deal by defining a joint purpose.*

Answer (D): Collaboration requires more than just working together. Creation of value starts with the framing of the common mission or joint purpose, commitment to that joint purpose and talent with no single entity dominating the discussion. Again, this is where we are discussing the collective "why."

Question 54: Newgotiation is rooted in:

    A. *Sharing and collaborating for better outcomes.*
    B. Producing deals that are time sensitive.
    C. Improvisation and intuition.
    D. Power, money and influence.

Answer (A): From all the negotiation pathologies and challenges we examined, practiced and taught none was superior to the technique and mindset we call Newgotiation. Newgotiation is rooted in sharing and collaborating as opposed to competing. Most negotiators see negotiation as a competitive arm wrestling in which 70% result in an impasse (0-0) and the remaining 30% with win-lose results (1-0) (2-1).

Question 55: Newgotiation can resolve every dispute.

A. True. As talking about price first then inventing options takes care of everything.
B. True. It is the best method known to mankind.
C. True. Being nice is always helpful.
D. *False. Negotiation is not a "silver or magic bullet" does not solve all problems but certainly provides a common language and framework to work hard for better results.*

Answer (D): We would be naïve to believe that Newgotiating can solve everything. Newgotiation is not about being just nice, cooperative and submissive all the time or being aggressive, assertive or competitive all the time. It is about all of those things balanced. Most of all it is a methodic process, a common language that if used correctly and diligently can yield remarkable results.

Question 56: Among others, Newgotiation extensively borrows from the literatures of:

A. Mathematics and physics.
B. *Collaborative governance and leadership.*
C. Reptilian Brian Science.
D. English literature.

Answer (B): Governance requires a different mindset and a collaborative effort to search for the common good. Successful governance is all about the quest for the win/win. The same can be said about leadership. Good Newgotiators have leadership qualities and in particular facilitative leadership qualities.

Question 57 Shared leadership generates:

A. More problems than it is worth.
B. Pricey products and services.
C. *More effective solutions in a rapidly changing world.*

D. Soft solutions

Answer (C): As in the case of collaborative governance today's complex problems require more than one actor or sector to creatively and effectively address or solve them. Shared leadership or shared facilitation through collaboration is more impactful and transformational.

Question 58 Good leaders:

A. Do not concern themselves with small problems.
B. Promote their own views.
C. *Give help by creating standards of excellence and setting an example for others to follow.*
D. Are egomaniacs.

Answer (C): Our prototypes of Newgotiators are good leaders. They give help by establishing principles concerning the way constituents, peers, colleagues and customers are treated. They give help modeling the way. They engage, listen, discern and act with rigor, discipline, accountability and transparency for everyone to win.

Question 59 Facilitative leaders provide:

A. Selective advice to others.
B. *Direction without controlling the way.*
C. Money to their friends only.
D. Answers to common problems.

Answer (B): Facilitative leaders are convinced that each person participating to the dialogue is holding a piece of the puzzle. Public facilitative leaders in particular are committed to collectively shaping the "why" knowing that it improves buy in from their constituents and substantially improve the chances of persuasive value creation and value distribution for the community at large.

Question 60: Our Newgotiation technique:

A. Promotes talking about price first then inventing options.

B. Invents one single option most useful to the most powerful negotiator.
C. Is always about being nice and never walk away from a deal.
D. *Improves the public value of a deal by inventing and good decision making.*

Answer (D): Our 4-10-10 Newgotiation Technique is a place to test options, analyze the context, make concessions, improve the relationships, manage power, reduce misunderstandings, respect rules, determine norms and manage time. Our Newgotiation Technique is a unified dialect, which helps organizations and individuals to create value and speak the same common language of Newgotiation by inventing and good decision making.